Improving Capacity for Stabilization and Reconstruction Operations

Nora Bensahel, Olga Oliker, Heather Peterson

Sponsored by the Office of the Secretary of Defense

 NATIONAL DEFENSE RESEARCH INSTITUTE

The research described in this report was conducted within the International Security and Defense Policy Center of the RAND National Defense Research Institute, a federally funded research and development center sponsored by the Office of the Secretary of Defense, the Joint Staff, the Unified Combatant Commands, the Department of the Navy, the Marine Corps, the defense agencies, and the defense Intelligence Community under Contract W74V8H-06-C-0002.

Library of Congress Cataloging-in-Publication Data is available for this publication.

978-0-8330-4698-7

Published 2009 by the RAND Corporation
1776 Main Street, P.O. Box 2138, Santa Monica, CA 90407-2138
1200 South Hayes Street, Arlington, VA 22202-5050
4570 Fifth Avenue, Suite 600, Pittsburgh, PA 15213-2665
RAND URL: http://www.rand.org/
To order RAND documents or to obtain additional information, contact
Distribution Services: Telephone: (310) 451-7002;
Fax: (310) 451-6915; Email: order@rand.org

Preface

Over the past few years, the United States and many of its allies and partners have become increasingly involved in stabilization and reconstruction operations around the world. Yet, ongoing efforts in Afghanistan, Iraq, and elsewhere have revealed major shortfalls in both the preparations for and execution of such operations that can undermine such operations' prospects for success. This book provides an overview of the requirements posed by stabilization and reconstruction operations and recommends ways to improve U.S. capacity for them.

This research was conducted within the International Security and Defense Policy Center of the RAND National Defense Research Institute, a federally funded research and development center sponsored by the Office of the Secretary of Defense, the Joint Staff, the Unified Combatant Commands, the Department of the Navy, the Marine Corps, the defense agencies, and the defense Intelligence Community.

For more information on RAND's International Security and Defense Policy Center, contact the Director, James Dobbins. He can be reached by email at dobbins@rand.org; by phone at (703) 413-1100, extension 5134; or by mail at the RAND Corporation, 1200 South Hayes Street, Arlington, VA 22202-5050. More information about RAND is available at www.rand.org.

Contents

Figure and Table

Figure

Table

Summary

Stabilization and reconstruction operations will almost certainly constitute an important part of the national security agenda facing the new Obama administration. Stabilization, which refers to efforts to end social, economic, and political upheaval, and reconstruction, which includes efforts to develop or redevelop institutions that foster self-governance, social and economic development, and security, are critical to securing political objectives before, during, or after conflict. Until recently, however, governments and militaries preferred to focus on conventional military operations. Skills and capacities for stabilization and reconstruction were either not fully developed or allowed to atrophy. This book provides an overview of the requirements posed by stabilization and reconstruction operations and recommends ways to improve U.S. capacity for them.

What Do Stabilization and Reconstruction Operations Entail?

Stabilization and reconstruction operations occur in places where host governments are weak or have lost the capacity to govern effectively. This means that those conducting such operations must assume, at least temporarily, many roles of the state while simultaneously trying to rebuild that capacity. Stabilization tasks, which are the highest priority, include such efforts as restoring law and order; providing humanitarian relief; supporting the disarmament, demobilization, and reintegration (DDR) of former combatants; and building or rebuilding local security capacity. Once these goals have been achieved, reconstruction tasks, such as building or rebuilding government institutions, promoting economic stabilization and development, and promoting democracy and representation, can be pursued.

These general stabilization and reconstruction tasks lead to specific U.S. capacity requirements:

- **Policing and the rule of law.** Since it is very unlikely that local civilian police will be capable of restoring law and order, stabilization operations require deployable civilian police, police trainers, and judicial and corrections experts.
- **Military and intelligence training and capacity building.** Military personnel can be used effectively for training the armed forces of the host country. U.S. and allied intelligence services usually take the lead in rebuilding intelligence capacity. However, both of these efforts require effective civilian and political oversight and appropriate levels of transparency.
- **DDR.** DDR efforts can be undertaken by either civilian or military personnel, but these efforts must be integrated into and flow from broader political reconciliation to be successful.
- **Humanitarian assistance.** If large-scale violence has forced key international organizations and nongovernmental organizations out of the country, then U.S. military and civilian personnel may be required to provide humanitarian assistance directly until the country is secure enough for the relief organizations to return. Otherwise, U.S. government personnel are more likely to be involved in coordinating international and domestic relief efforts than in providing direct assistance.
- **Governance, democratization, and human rights.** In the immediate aftermath of conflict, U.S. personnel may have to help govern the host country. Over time, they can move into an advisory role vis-à-vis indigenous personnel. Relevant expertise exists throughout the U.S. government, but not in a deployable form.

Recent Efforts to Build Capacity

In the past few years, the U.S. government has undertaken a number of important initiatives to build the capacities identified above. The most important of these steps is the creation within the State Department of the Office of the Coordinator for Reconstruction and Stabilization (S/CRS), whose mission is to coordinate and lead U.S. government efforts to plan, prepare, and conduct stabilization and reconstruction operations. In addition to chairing interagency working groups, S/CRS has developed a planning framework that guides the development of civilian plans for stabilization and reconstruction. It has also developed an interagency management system for operating in crises. When fully implemented, this system will include a policy-coordination group, a civilian planning cell, and deployable civilian teams.

S/CRS's most ambitious effort to date is the Civilian Stabilization Initiative, which includes a deployable civilian capacity called the Civilian Response Corps. As planned, the Corps will include three components:

- an *active* component composed of 250 full-time U.S. government personnel from eight U.S. agencies who are available to deploy within 24 hours
- a *standby* component composed of 2,000 personnel from the same eight agencies who would receive stabilization and reconstruction training and be deployable within 30 days for up to six months
- a *reserve* component composed of 2,000 personnel from the private sector and state and local governments who have unique skills not found in the federal government.

The biggest problem with the Civilian Response Corps is that Congress has only recently started allocating the funds to make it fully operational.

Other U.S. government initiatives to improve capacity for stabilization and reconstruction operations include the National Security Professional Development Program, which combines several initiatives to encourage familiarization with stabilization and reconstruction operations and closer cooperation among U.S. government civilian personnel. The U.S. Agency for International Development (USAID) has also adopted a number of initiatives to improve its capacity in these areas, including the creation of a new Office of Military Affairs to facilitate USAID coordination with U.S. and foreign military personnel. The Department of Defense (DoD) is also institutionalizing new processes for managing its deployable civilians.

A number of significant challenges remain, however. There have been several new interagency strategies, plans, and initiatives in the U.S. government in recent years, but there has been little effort to rationalize and prioritize them. A huge funding mismatch between DoD and the rest of the civilian agencies involved in such operations persists. This disparity has perpetuated the lack of deployable civilian capacity and has led the military to take on many of these missions by default. No fewer than eight separate congressional committees deal with stabilization and reconstruction issues, which makes coordinating funding a particular challenge. And neither the United States nor its most frequent global partners have enough capacity to meet the demands for deployable police forces in these operations. While rhetoric about the importance of nonmilitary capabilities has grown, funding and capabilities have remained small compared to the challenge.

Recommendations

Many reports have been written on stabilization and reconstruction during the past few years. All agree on the need for increased civilian capacity and better interagency coordination. However, there is less agreement about exactly how to implement those changes. The following list offers several broad themes that should guide decisions on capacity development and suggests ways ahead that can help reconcile priorities, resources, and capabilities in the years to come:

- **Emphasize civilian rather than military capabilities.** Although many initiatives are under way to build civilian capacity within other branches of the U.S. government, there is also a significant effort under way in DoD to develop reconstruction and stabilization capabilities. If the development of military capacities in DoD continues to outpace the development of civilian capabilities in the State Department and USAID, DoD will continue to lead stabilization and reconstruction operations by default. This continuing trend would weaken the State Department and strengthen the perception that the U.S. military is the nation's primary instrument of power. This could be harmful to perceptions of U.S. aid efforts globally. The trend would also likely prove ineffective, since most of the knowledge and expertise for these missions lies outside the military.

- **Realign National Security Council, State, and USAID roles.** While it is tempting to build new agencies or rearrange organizational charts to address the interagency challenges of stabilization and reconstruction, reforming existing agencies may make more sense. The National Security Council (NSC) should be responsible for interagency coordination for stabilization and reconstruction, since its primary mission is to coordinate the nation's foreign and security policies. The NSC, however, is poorly resourced and structured to define detailed strategies and policies. The State Department may be better suited to play this role from an organizational perspective. However, it has very little large-scale expeditionary capability, and it does not control the majority of programs and capabilities necessary to actually conduct stabilization and reconstruction operations.

  USAID is the organization that makes the most sense to take the lead in these operations. It already has an expeditionary culture, and it controls the majority of the programs related to stabilization and reconstruction. USAID capabilities would require significant upgrading and development to allow the agency to take on the lead role in stabilization and reconstruction operations without overtaking its existing mandate. These changes would require transformation of recruiting, training, management, and deployment in addition to significant new resources.

- **Fund and implement the Civilian Stabilization Initiative.** The Civilian Stabilization Initiative is currently the U.S. government's most important effort to build civilian capacity, but it has never been fully funded. The new administration should work closely with Congress to convince the relevant appropriations committees that relatively small investments in these areas will provide large returns in ensuring that the U.S. government can adequately respond to the challenges of stabilization and reconstruction. Once this happens, bureaucratic challenges associated with implementing such funding decisions will undoubtedly arise, especially regarding trade-offs with capacity at the state and local levels.

- **Improve deployable police capacity.** This capacity requires special attention because of its significant requirements in terms of both capabilities and numbers of personnel. Some current and former police officers already serve in these types of operations, but using currently serving police officers on a large scale poses numerous problems. If the U.S. government is serious about expanding its deployable police capacity, it will need to find ways to encourage police departments around the country—as well as individual police officers themselves—to participate. The National Guard and Reserves and Urban Search and Rescue Teams may be able to serve as models.

- **Improve management for stabilization and reconstruction.** The State Department and USAID have focused on improving day-to-day and strategic management, but they have paid less attention to crisis management. This involves identifying potential missions that the United States will undertake, building sufficient capacity for such missions, planning for potential missions, and implementing crisis-management processes.

- **Ensure coherent guidance and funding for effectiveness and sustainability.** Building capacity for stabilization and reconstruction means not only developing the right approach but also making sure that approach can be implemented. This means that (1) the legal and bureaucratic framework has to reflect efforts under way, (2) resources must be allocated as needed, and (3) the new institutions can outlast individual administrations. Directives such as National Security Presidential Directive–44, Management of Interagency Efforts Concerning Reconstruction and Stabilization, are important but not themselves sufficient. Presidential-level guidance must be the source of a coherent and consistent package of regulations and rules that creates a new, effective system. Presidential guidance must be coordinated with congressional guidance, both in defining missions and tasks and in allocating resources.

Acknowledgments

The authors wish to thank Marc Cheek, Joe Collins, Keith Crane, Jim Dobbins, and Greg Hermsmeyer for their comments on earlier drafts of this book. Any errors or omissions in this book should, of course, be attributed to the authors alone.

Abbreviations

ACT	Advance Civilian Team
AFRICOM	U.S. Africa Command
CAFC	Commission for Assistance to a Free Cuba
CIVPOL	civilian police
COCOM	Combatant Command
COESPU	Center of Excellence for Stability Police Units
COM	chief of mission
CPA	Coalition Provisional Authority
CRSG	Country Reconstruction and Stabilization Group
DART	Disaster Assistance Response Team [USAID]
DCHA	Bureau of Democracy, Conflict, and Humanitarian Assistance [USAID]
DDR	disarmament, demobilization, and reintegration
DHS	Department of Homeland Security
DoD	Department of Defense
DPKO	Department of Peacekeeping Operations [UN]

DUSD(CPP)	Deputy Under Secretary of Defense for Civilian Personnel Policy
FACT	Field Advance Civilian Team
FY	fiscal year
IDP	internally displaced person
IMS	Interagency Management System
INL	Bureau of International Narcotics and Law Enforcement Affairs [State]
IO	international organization
IPC	Integration Planning Cell
JIACG	Joint Interagency Coordination Group
MP	military police
NGO	nongovernmental organization
NSC	National Security Council
NSPD	National Security Presidential Directive
OFDA	Office of Foreign Disaster Assistance [USAID]
OMA	Office of Military Affairs [USAID]
OPM	Office of Personnel Management
OTI	Office of Transition Initiatives [USAID]
PCC	Policy Coordinating Committee
PDD	Presidential Decision Directive
PRT	Provincial Reconstruction Team
S/CRS	Office of the Coordinator for Reconstruction and Stabilization [State]
SOUTHCOM	U.S. Southern Command

SWAT	Special Weapons and Tactics
UN	United Nations
USAID	U.S. Agency for International Development
USAR	Urban Search and Rescue [USAID]

CHAPTER ONE

Why Stabilization and Reconstruction?

The experiences of the United States in Iraq and Afghanistan in recent years have underlined the importance of stabilization by demonstrating that ending conflict is not as easy as planners may have expected upon first undertaking military operations. These experiences have helped feed a debate over the role of stabilization and reconstruction—and, thus, just how much capacity the United States and other countries need to carry out these missions—in U.S. strategic interests in the 21st century.

Specifically, the wars in Iraq and Afghanistan have bolstered arguments that efforts to advance political and economic development in countries experiencing conflict or emerging from it—that, is reconstruction—are crucial to U.S. national security. This is argued to be true both in cases in which the United States is involved in the conflict (as in World War II, Vietnam, Iraq, and Afghanistan) and those in which the United States becomes involved explicitly to end the conflict and assist in the rebuilding process (as in the Balkans, Somalia, and Liberia). Thus, to effectively advance national security goals, the United States needs to improve its capacity for stabilization and reconstruction operations.

Two fundamental assumptions drive most arguments that stabilization and reconstruction operations are and will continue to be crucial to national security. The first is that global conflict and underdevelopment are national security threats because they spur radicalism and spread violence. The second is that by providing assistance to stabilize and promote development in countries experiencing conflict or emerging from it, the United States enhances its credibility in these countries and globally, thus strengthening U.S. influence and building lasting ties. Those who argue that a component of reconstruction activities involves the development of effective and democratic governance may also argue that these changes, in turn, make future alignment with the United States more likely.

These assumptions, and their increasing acceptance by policymakers, reflect a shift in how conflict and security are viewed both by governments and their citizens. This shift began in the last half of the 20th century and continues today, a fact manifested by interventions geared specifically to end human suffering, such as those undertaken in the Balkans and Somalia and called for today in Sudan.

This change in perceptions has not stemmed from any changes in the realities of security. Instead, it reflects a better understanding of the repercussions and dynamics of insecurity. Again and again, those who have fought insurgencies have learned that they cannot win without public support and that they cannot gain that support without improving and protecting local lives and livelihoods. People will blame those in power for the deaths of their loved ones. Whether their loved ones die of a bullet or lack of potable water matters less than which government or occupying force caused—or failed to prevent—a preventable death. The lesson of Iraq and Afghanistan for U.S. and allied forces, just like the lessons of past wars, is that stabilization and reconstruction cannot be ignored when fighting a conflict.

Although this lesson may have been learned before, governments and militaries preferred until quite recently to think of such operations as outliers and to focus instead on so-called conventional warfare. As a result, skills and capacities for stabilization and reconstruction were not fully developed, and those that did exist atrophied. Then, when they proved relevant and necessary once again, they had to be rebuilt. The shift in perceptions we see today provides an opportunity to truly learn the lessons of the past and adapt accordingly so that future efforts will be more effective.

This book provides an overview of the requirements posed by stabilization and reconstruction operations and recommends ways to improve U.S. capacity to meet them. It begins by defining *stabilization* and *reconstruction*, terms that are often used inconsistently and inaccurately. It then considers the evolution of U.S. views and discusses the various actors involved in such operations. Chapter Two examines what stabilization and reconstruction operations entail, including both their operational and planning requirements. Chapter Three summarizes recent U.S. efforts to build capacity, noting what has been accomplished so far as well as some challenges that remain. Chapter Four concludes the book by recommending several additional initiatives that the new administration should undertake to improve U.S. capacity in this important area.

What Are Stabilization and Reconstruction?

The family of efforts grouped together under stabilization and reconstruction encompasses a range of overlapping missions that are themselves components of a broad range of different engagements and approaches. Stabilization, for example, generally refers to the effort to end conflict and social, economic, and political upheaval. Stability in each of these spheres is necessary for effective reconstruction because without it, any gains will be short-lived.

Stabilization, thus defined, is one component of a wide range of possible operations. For example, stabilization can be carried out as part of an intervention. Indeed, it can be the express purpose of an intervention to end violence. It is also crucial in the aftermath of combat operations, which may have intentionally or unintentionally helped spur additional conflict. Stabilization is also an accepted component of counterinsurgency operations because efforts to gain local support, which are so central to counterinsurgency, generally require ending violence and upheaval. Counterterrorism operations may also include a stabilization component. For example, if these operations take place in an unstable environment, stabilization may be critical to gathering intelligence. Definitionally, stabilization is part and parcel of postconflict operations and necessary for any sort of nation-building efforts to take place.

Reconstruction refers to the process of developing or redeveloping structures that permit sustainable self-government, social and economic development, and security. Reconstruction picks up where stabilization leaves off in any and all of the sorts of operations just described. This is why stabilization is a necessary precondition for reconstruction: Without it, subsequent efforts are not sustainable. Although some reconstruction and stabilization efforts coincide, the former cannot succeed without the latter.

In the context of violent conflict, these two families of tasks play different roles. Stabilization is, by definition, the key to ending violence. Reconstruction, by contrast, is believed to help prevent a return to violence by addressing longer-term drivers of violent conflict. Although reconstruction and stabilization tasks are distinct, they affect each other in important ways. Once basic security has been established, reconstruction tasks are critical to eliminating many of the factors that can drive further violence. By ensuring that a society and an economy grow, reconstruction gives people and their leaders the stake in a nonviolent future that is crucial to building that future. Chapter Two further defines the specific tasks that fall under stabilization and reconstruction missions.

Who Conducts Stabilization and Reconstruction Tasks?

A large number of different groups and individuals are likely to be involved in stabilization and reconstruction operations: U.S. and foreign military forces, U.S. and foreign government personnel, local officials and actors, and a host of others. This fact presents U.S. government actors with both benefits and challenges. On one hand, a variety of global and host-country actors have capabilities the United States does not and can thus fill key gaps. On the other, some actors are hostile to and work at cross-purposes with U.S. goals. Moreover, friendly actors create challenging coordination and cooperation requirements as well as the basic need for mutual awareness. Some of the actors likely to be involved in various stabilization and reconstruction tasks are identified below.[1]

U.S. Military Personnel

The military will play a substantial role in many U.S. stabilization and reconstruction missions, either because military forces have been deployed to end violence or because they have been party to the violence in the first place. Recognition of this reality, made even more apparent by ongoing efforts in Iraq and Afghanistan, has led the Department of Defense (DoD) to incorporate stabilization and reconstruction into U.S. military doctrine as substantial and growing components. Stabilization and reconstruction tasks align all but perfectly with the body of tasks that the U.S. military describes as stability operations.[2] According to U.S. military doctrine,[3] stability operations include both shorter- and longer-term tasks. The former ensure security for the local population, restore essential services, and meet humanitarian needs. The latter develop indigenous capacity to secure essential services and assist in the development of a viable market economy, the rule of law, democratic institutions, and a robust civil society. The shorter-term tasks are thus stabilization tasks; the longer-term ones are those geared toward reconstruction.

Stability operations, once considered to be a lesser-included case of major combat operations, have become increasingly central to DoD

---

[1] This list and discussion draw from Keith Crane, Olga Oliker, Nora Bensahel, Derek Eaton, S. Jamie Gayton, Brooke Stearns Lawson, Jeffrey Martini, John L. Nasir, Michelle Parker, Jerry M. Sollinger, and Kayla M. Williams, *Guidebook for Providing Economic Assistance at the Tactical Level During Stability Operations*, Santa Monica, Calif.: RAND Corporation, TR-633-A, 2009.

[2] Joint Chiefs of Staff, Joint Publication 1-02, *DoD Dictionary of Military and Associated Terms*, April 12, 2001, as amended through October 17, 2008, defines *stability operations* as

> an overarching term encompassing various military missions, tasks, and activities conducted outside the United States in coordination with other instruments of national power to maintain or reestablish a safe and secure environment, provide essential government services, emergency infrastructure reconstruction, and humanitarian relief.

[3] Stability operations doctrine is formally documented in Headquarters, Department of the Army, Field Manual 3-07, *Stability Operations*, October 2008, and Joint Chiefs of Staff, Joint Publication 3-0, *Operations*, September 2006.

planning and doctrine. The U.S. military now considers stability oper-
ations to be a core mission just as important as combat operations.[4]
Military forces train and plan for stability operations, doctrine focuses
on the core tasks involved, and resources are allocated for related tasks.
In fact, two U.S. Combatant Commands (COCOMs), U.S. Southern
Command (SOUTHCOM) and the nascent U.S. Africa Command
(AFRICOM), are more focused on building security relationships and
preventing conflict than on combat operations.

Military doctrine also emphasizes the complementarity of stability operations and counterinsurgency and related missions. Indeed,
counterinsurgency is defined as requiring offensive operations, defen-
sive operations, and stability operations.[5] As noted, both stabilization and reconstruction can support counterinsurgency, and effective
counterinsurgency operations make stabilization and reconstruction
possible. Some of the same tasks are undertaken in support of all three.
The three terms, however, are not synonymous, and the operations are
not fully aligned. Many stabilization and reconstruction missions are
undertaken in places where no counterinsurgency efforts are necessary,
and some counterinsurgency efforts take place in areas that are otherwise comparatively stable and prosperous and thus require little in the
way of stabilization and reconstruction.

Although the military has increasingly embraced the stability
operations mission, it recognizes that many of the tasks in question
are rarely traditional military ones. Indeed, the military doctrine cited
above states that the military role in such operations is a support role.
Civilian actors are considered better capable of carrying out most of the
core tasks, which are not traditional military missions. In fact, when
security is defined more broadly, only a small part of it is amenable to
traditional military solutions, as is discussed in detail in Chapter Two.
At the same time, doctrinal documents indicate that U.S. military

---

[4] See U.S. Department of Defense, Directive 3000.05, *Military Support for Stability, Security, Transition, and Reconstruction (SSTR) Operations*, November 28, 2005; Headquarters,
Department of the Army, Field Manual 3-0, *Operations*, February 2008; and Joint Publication 3-0, *Joint Operations*.

[5] Headquarters, Department of the Army, Field Manual 3-24, *Counterinsurgency: The Army
and Marine Corps Field Manual on Counterinsurgency*, December 2006.

personnel must be prepared to perform all tasks required to establish stability when civilians cannot do so. Indeed, in ongoing operations in Iraq and Afghanistan, military personnel are carrying out the full range of stabilization and operations missions.

U.S. Government Civilians

If there is broad agreement that most stabilization and reconstruction tasks are better carried out by civilians, why is the military doing so much, and why are civilians in such short supply for these missions? The reasons are rooted in the fact that although stabilization and reconstruction have become integrated into how the United States views warfare and national security, the institutions of government were structured during the late Cold War era, when these issues were a lower priority. Thus, the State Department and the U.S. Agency for International Development (USAID)—the government agencies best capable, in terms of both mission and capacity, of carrying out nonmilitary stabilization and reconstruction tasks—are not configured for effective, large-scale, rapid deployment. Although the State Department mission of diplomacy and the USAID mission of economic-capacity development make those agencies the right actors in principle, neither agency has access to substantial numbers of qualified personnel that can be rapidly moved across the world. Funding for foreign aid in 1949 was roughly equal to the DoD budget at the time, but U.S. spending on international security and development programs was by 2006 just one-thirteenth the size of the Pentagon budget, even excluding the costs of the war in Iraq.[6] Indeed, USAID's ranks were five times larger during the Vietnam War than they are now.[7]

Moreover, hands-on development efforts managed by the State Department and USAID are, for the most part, carried out through nongovernmental organizations (NGOs) and other contractors rather

---

[6] Charles A. Stevenson, *Warriors and Politicians: US Civil-Military Relations Under Stress,* New York: Routledge, 2006, p. 118.

[7] USAID employed as many as 15,000 personnel during the Vietnam War. It employs approximately 3,000 personnel today. See Robert M. Gates, "A Balanced Strategy: Reprogramming the Pentagon for a New Age," *Foreign Affairs,* Vol. 88, No. 1, January/February 2009.

than by U.S. government staff. Although both agencies have at their disposal staff who can serve as advisors to foreign governments and institutions, as well as personnel who can play planning and government roles, actual development projects and substantial training efforts are generally implemented by contractors. Although there are exceptions, notably within USAID's Office of Foreign Disaster Assistance (OFDA), this structural bias adds a layer of effort and bureaucracy to any planned action and exacerbates the problems of deployability.[8]

U.S. government civilian personnel are further subject to a variety of restrictions developed to guarantee their security. These restrictions often prevent civilians from deploying to conflict areas or constrain their movements when they do deploy. DoD, by contrast, is configured precisely for going quickly and in large numbers to dangerous parts of the world. Finally, of course, if a conflict is under way, military personnel are already there.

This is not to say that State and USAID neither have people to deploy nor are willing deploy to a stabilization and reconstruction operation. They do and they will. Other government agencies can also contribute personnel according to their specializations and needs, as discussed in the succeeding chapters. However, these agencies do not have the capacity to contribute substantial quantities of staff.

U.S. Government Contractors

In addition to government personnel, the U.S. government and its agencies may employ contractors to carry out a variety of tasks. These tasks can include support functions, such as providing food, logistics, and security services for U.S. personnel (e.g., through bodyguards), and reconstruction tasks, such as organizing and carrying out construction.[9] Contractors have also been used for policing and police training in some operations. Contractors may be hired individually or through

---

[8] See Chapter Three for further discussion of USAID's role in stabilization and reconstruction.

[9] This reliance on contractors is not limited to U.S. government civilian agencies. The U.S. military has also become increasingly dependent on contractors in recent years, even for such military tasks as operating and maintaining weapon platforms.

a contracting corporation. The use of contractors is controversial, particularly when their tasks overlap with those of U.S. government representatives. A good deal of U.S.-funded development work around the world, however, is carried out through contracts signed with for-profit and not-for-profit organizations.

The Host-Nation Government at the National and Local Levels, Possibly Including Security Personnel

The host-nation government is the most important partner for the United States in stabilization and reconstruction. Indeed, it is the lead partner of the United States during all of these efforts. The more capable it is, the more it can provide security, governance, and development itself. The less capable it is, the more assistance it will need in carrying out these functions. Stabilization success depends on improving local capacity, transferring genuine (not just formal) control as soon as feasible, and ensuring that U.S. efforts support host-nation sovereignty and host-nation goals. Developing local capacity must therefore be at the core of all U.S. efforts. Even before operations, all plans and efforts need to be coordinated with host-government plans and consistent with local codes, laws, and regulations.

Civilian and Military Branches of Other Countries Involved in the Postconflict Effort

The United States may not be the only country that has sent forces to the area of operations. It usually acts in cooperation with other countries that also deploy military forces, civilian staff, or both. Hostile states may also send their own personnel. Different states take different approaches to stabilization and reconstruction, and their military and diplomatic missions face the task of deconflicting efforts and ensuring complementarity. Lacking substantial numbers of deployable civilians for key tasks, most states face the same problems the United States does. Some, however, have capabilities that the United States lacks, and vice-versa.

International Organizations

International organizations (IOs), such as the United Nations (UN), the World Bank, and other development banks, have significant capacity to assist in stabilization and reconstruction efforts. All have expertise and deployable capacity for various economic stabilization and development tasks. The UN's Department of Peacekeeping Operations (DPKO), for example, manages one of the largest deployed forces in the world.[10] In addition to peacekeeping and related efforts, the UN has capacity for international policing; disarmament, demobilization, and reintegration (DDR); and developing governance. However, the extent to which these actors are deployed and available will vary according to the specific circumstances of any given mission.

International and Local Nongovernmental Organizations

NGOs, such as Mercy Corps and Oxfam, are not-for-profit organizations that work either locally or globally. Many concentrate on specific issues, such as humanitarian assistance, development, health care, migration, and human rights. International NGOs deploy foreign staff, hire locally, and work primarily at the community level. Local NGOs are based and staffed locally. NGOs have capacity for humanitarian assistance, development, and some governance tasks. Some NGOs accept government contracts and can carry out tasks that U.S. government personnel cannot conduct. In some cases, such NGOs may also be performing those tasks without a government contract. Under conditions of significant violence, some international NGOs will be unable to deploy, and some local and international NGOs will be unable to work. In conflict situations, NGOs may seek to avoid the appearance of cooperation and collaboration with the U.S. government (and particularly the U.S. military). Much progress has been made in recent years in defining interactions between NGOs and military forces in

---

[10] In December 2008, DPKO managed more than 91,000 deployed military and police forces. See United Nations Peacekeeping, "Monthly Summary of Contributors of Military and Civilian Police Personnel, 2009," Web page, 2009.

areas where both are active, as they will be in most stabilization and reconstruction operations.[11]

The Humanitarian Arms of International Political Groups, Including Those That Are Violent and Radical (Such as Hizbollah)

Groups hostile to the stability operation, the host-nation government, or the United States and its coalition partners may try to undermine U.S. stabilization and reconstruction efforts. For example, they may violently target individuals involved in U.S. efforts. At the same time, they may also carry out competing stabilization and reconstruction programs or even claim credit for U.S. and local-government efforts. Development assistance carried out by such groups creates particular challenges for the United States and the host nation because such aid usually meets important needs that might not otherwise be met. The best counter to such efforts is developing strong and effective relations with the host-nation government and communities, particularly at the local level.

International and Multinational Businesses

As a situation stabilizes, international businesses will, it is to be hoped, become interested in operating in the developing local economy. Their involvement can be an important factor in long-term reconstruction success.

Local Social and Civil-Society Organizations and Businesses

Important local actors include government officials, the religious community, tribal leaders, teachers, and the business community. Each may play a role in stabilization and reconstruction efforts. Outreach and coordination at the local level can be critical to success because local leaders know what their communities need and local economic actors will be the ones to effect growth.

---

[11] See United States Institute of Peace, *Guidelines for Relations Between U.S. Armed Forces and Non-Governmental Humanitarian Organizations in Hostile or Potentially Hostile Environments,* c. 2007. The DoD and key NGOs have agreed to these guidelines.

The Challenge of Building and Leveraging Capacity

To be effective, future stabilization and reconstruction operations will require a combination of new capabilities and improvements to the ways in which existing capabilities are utilized. Challenges of coordination within and outside the U.S. government also need to be overcome. In today's security environment, however, it would be folly for the U.S. government to take anything but a proactive role in defining mission requirements and developing ways to meet those requirements. How the U.S. government chooses to (1) plan for and carry out stabilization and reconstruction missions, (2) determine which stabilization and reconstruction missions will be undertaken, and which will not, and (3) prioritize stabilization and reconstruction in the context of other national security goals and missions will shape the United States' future global role and capabilities.

CHAPTER TWO

What Do Stabilization and Reconstruction Operations Entail?

By their nature, stabilization and reconstruction operations are complex undertakings that involve activities in many different issue areas and require extensive coordination among the wide range of actors identified in the previous chapter. Specific requirements will vary in different operations. Some operations will occur after conflict has ended, while others may be designed to prevent conflict from erupting in the first place. Some operations will occur under conditions of insurgency and continuing violence, while others may be more peaceful. Some operations will rely heavily on military personnel, while others may involve more civilian and nongovernmental actors because of requirements and capacity constraints. Despite these differences, there are certain recurring issues that most stabilization and reconstruction operations will have to address. This chapter identifies some of the most important operational requirements in key areas and then examines some of the planning needs associated with these requirements.

Operational Requirements

Stabilization and reconstruction operations occur in places where host governments are weak or have lost the capacity to govern effectively. Those conducting such operations must often assume, at least temporarily, many roles of the state while simultaneously trying to rebuild that capacity.

As discussed in Chapter One, stabilization tasks that build and ensure peace and stability will be the most immediately crucial during operations in which violence remains endemic. Once some stability has been achieved, reconstruction tasks, such as the development and establishment of democratic government, can be pursued.[1] Economic growth and development are impossible without security, and building an effective government while under fire is an equally insurmountable task. Thus, investments in reconstruction may be wasted if stabilization needs are not adequately addressed.[2]

This does not mean that longer-term reconstruction efforts cannot be pursued until there is complete security. It means that for other reconstruction efforts to succeed, security must come first and be a consistent focus throughout. That said, efforts to improve security, meet immediate humanitarian needs, and otherwise stabilize the situation must be undertaken with an eye to longer-term goals. The need for longer-term economic sustainability, civilian control of security forces, and effective indigenous governance must govern the ways in which stability is provided. Efforts to stabilize the situation in the near-term must be tailored to minimize the chances that such efforts will lead to longer-term destabilization (e.g., by exacerbating tensions between communities).

Security: The Military, the Police, and the Rule of Law

Immediate Law and Order. Providing security for the local population is the single most important task during stabilization and reconstruction operations. Unless basic order prevails, none of the other tasks can make lasting contributions. If the operation follows a military conflict or seeks to end one, the first few weeks provide a critical opportunity to shape future conditions. During this period, which is often called the *golden hour*, intervening forces need to ensure that law

---

[1]   This section relies heavily on James Dobbins, Seth G. Jones, Keith Crane, and Beth Cole DeGrasse, *The Beginner's Guide to Nation Building*, Santa Monica, Calif.: RAND Corporation, MG-557-SRF, 2007, although we disagree with the authors on some specific issues.

[2]   Dobbins et al., 2007, pp. 13–15.

and order prevail and that looters, former combatants, criminals, and potential insurgents cannot take advantage of a chaotic situation.

Disarmament, Demobilization, and Reintegration. Another component of stabilization is ensuring that there is a political solution that enables former combatants to agree to eschew the use of force. Until the security situation is stabilized effectively, it is highly unlikely that any effort to disarm, demobilize, and reintegrate former combatants will succeed. As long as force is either politically effective or viewed as critical for self-protection and group protection, combatants and their leaders will not lay down arms.

Once there is a political agreement to end violence, DDR efforts are critical to cementing the peace. Former combatants can be a particularly destabilizing force: Without successful DDR, they retain arms and can therefore threaten or use violence to secure their own interests. A well-designed DDR process helps get weapons off the streets (at least heavy, military-grade weapons, even in places where light arms are widely held) and helps fighters become productive members of society who have a stake in cementing the new political order rather than challenging it from the outside.

The reintegration component of DDR often incorporates the development of sustainable employment and educational opportunities for former combatants. These opportunities reduce incentives for resuming violent activities and contribute to overall development. DDR specifics will vary according to the situation. For example, if a conflict has been long-standing, combatants may be isolated from their communities and see few alternatives to violence. Reintegrating them into communities and developing opportunities for their employment and education will be critical to the success of the program. When combatant groups have recruited large numbers of children, DDR programs must include components specifically targeted at those children. Past experience indicates that such efforts should neither attempt to mainstream these children with children who have not seen combat nor attempt to integrate them into programs designed for former adult combatants. Similarly, gender, ethnic, and minority issues must also be considered in the design of DDR programs.

DDR provides an excellent example of how near-term stabilization efforts can backfire in the long term if not properly designed. Even when apparently successful in the disarmament and demobilization phases, DDR efforts have encountered challenges in effectively reintegrating former combatants. This is due in part to the long-term nature of the reintegration process, the need for sustained assistance and donor support, and the need for local economic development to move forward in a way that absorbs former combatants.[3] The impact of reintegration failure can be profound because the economic displacement of a substantial population that is trained in violence is detrimental to long-term security and economic development.

Building or Rebuilding Local Security Capacity. Just as a failure to effectively implement the reintegration component of DDR can undermine stabilization efforts, a strategy of using only foreign forces to provide security without undertaking a commensurate effort to develop and improve the capacity of local security forces will fail in the longer term. The host nation will eventually have to provide its own security, and this should begin as soon as possible. Building up local security capacity makes it possible for U.S. forces to draw down, whereas not doing so entails risks. For example, the longer the host country's public relies on foreigners for stability, the less trust it will have in its own government and the more it will tend to view the foreign presence as an occupation. Such distrust and frustration can open the way for competing groups to revert to violence to seek political control.

The development of local security capacity will usually involve extensive training of local military forces and, most importantly, local

---

[3] For discussions of these challenges, see, for example, Lotta Hagman and Zoe Nielsen, *A Framework for Lasting Disarmament, Demobilization, and Reintegration of Former Combatants in Crisis Situations,* International Peace Academy IPA Workshop Report, December 31, 2002; Béatrice Pouligny, *The Politics and Anti-Politics of Contemporary "Disarmament, Demobilization & Reintegration" Programs,* Paris/New York/Geneva: CERI/SGDN/PSIS, September 2004; Robert Muggah, "No Magic Bullet: A Critical Perspective on Disarmament, Demobilization and Reintegration (DDR) and Weapons Reduction in Post-Conflict Contexts," *The Round Table,* Vol. 94, No. 379, April 2005, pp. 239–252; and United Nations Interagency Working Group on Disarmament, Demobilization, and Reintegration, "Briefing Note for Senior Managers on the Integrated Disarmament, Demobilization, and Reintegration Standards," undated.

police. This process will be particularly challenging in countries whose previous security forces were highly politicized or nonexistent. It will typically include the development of other security functions, such as intelligence, although these can be lower-priority tasks. The design of the security sector should reflect the near- and long-term needs of the host country, an effort that will require a comprehensive assessment of needs.

No less important is the fact that establishing lasting security requires extensive efforts to rebuild judicial and corrections systems. It does not matter if the police forces are the best in the world if there are no judges to hear cases and no jails and prisons in which the accused and the guilty can be held. Judicial and corrections systems must often be reformed or rebuilt during stabilization and reconstruction operations —often at the same time that police forces are being retrained or reconstituted—to ensure that those who are arrested can have their cases fairly adjudicated rather than being released simply because there are no functioning courts or prisons.

Efforts to train the host-country military must take into account two key potential dangers. The first is the danger of building the military force the United States seeks rather than the one the host country needs. Force development and training should be based on a careful evaluation, with host-country guidance, of the country's key threats, how its choices will be perceived by neighbors, and so forth. Military forces should not be built solely to replace U.S. forces when they transition out—they should be built with an eye toward long-term needs. Otherwise, long-term needs will not be met, and the force that is built will prove inadequate or counterproductive.

The second danger to avoid is using the new military domestically as a police force. Because the foreign military is present and can effectively train other military forces, and because police trainers are usually absent in large numbers,[4] comparatively effective local military capabilities will often emerge before local police capabilities become available. This creates a strong incentive to utilize the newly trained military forces in police capacities because doing so replaces U.S. and other

---

[4]   Like other civilians, they are generally more difficult to recruit and deploy.

foreign forces on the street with local security personnel. Although getting foreigners off the street is clearly an important goal, replacing them with local military forces can be dangerous. Military training and approaches are fundamentally different from those appropriate for community police or paramilitary or special-operations police needed for counterinsurgency, counterterrorism, and other specialized missions. Local military personnel, particularly those who have been recently and rapidly trained, will not know how to carry out policing duties in a way that makes local people feel safe and secure. Moreover, the use of local military forces as police sets a dangerous precedent of using the military domestically, a practice that is often a forerunner to autocratic and violent rule (and is certainly not in keeping with democratic principles).

The key issues for intelligence-sector development are ensuring that such efforts are appropriately integrated into the development of the broader security sector and the government and that both U.S. and host-nation leaders have a clear sense of goals and processes. Just as the United States must design the military the host nation requires, it must resist the temptation to build the intelligence capacity it seeks rather than the one the host nation needs.

Throughout the security sector, efforts cannot stop simply at recruiting and training police, military personnel, lawyers, judges, prison guards, intelligence personnel, and analysts. They also require building ministries so that the host government develops the capacity to manage and oversee its security forces. Building ministerial capacity must be integrated into the broader process of developing the government. Security ministries and forces have to be built in a way that contributes to overall efforts to assure civilian control, oversight, accountability, respect for human rights, and democratic governance. Otherwise, such ministries and forces can undermine those efforts and the country's longer-term success.

A substantial body of literature on security-sector development, which focuses on both postconflict and more-peaceful developing countries, can be drawn on during these security efforts.[5]

Humanitarian Assistance and Displacement

Most stabilization and reconstruction operations occur in areas where civilian populations need some degree of assistance. Operations that occur in a postconflict environment—or in the midst of continuing violence—will likely face the greatest humanitarian needs. Humanitarian assistance is provided to save lives and alleviate suffering caused by conflict. Conflict creates poverty and limits people's access to food, water, shelter, and health care. It also cuts supply lines, leading to starvation and disease. Food, water, shelter, and medical care are usually the most immediate requirements.

It is critical that all forms of humanitarian assistance be given to anyone who needs them. Failure to do so is likely to have negative repercussions for long-term stabilization and development by dividing the country and perpetuating suffering. Moreover, international humanitarian law and practice prohibit aid providers from withholding humanitarian aid or using it to reward or punish individuals or groups.[6]

---

[5] A broad range of literature looks at specific experiences in various countries. A good general overview and source material for key topics can be found in Global Facilitation Network for Security Sector Reform, *A Beginner's Guide to Security Sector Reform*, Birmingham, UK, 2007; United Kingdom Department for International Development, *Understanding and Supporting Security Sector Reform*, London, 2002; David C. Gompert, Olga Oliker, and Anga Timilsina, *Clean, Lean and Able: A Strategy for Defense Sector Development*, Santa Monica, Calif.: RAND Corporation, OP-101-RC, 2004; Albrecht Schnabel and Hans-Georg Ehrhart, eds., *Security Sector Reform and Post-Conflict Peacebuilding*, Tokyo: United Nations University Press, 2005; and the work of Nicole Ball.

[6] The Fourth Geneva Convention and the First and Second 1977 protocols to the Geneva Conventions require combatants to ensure the provision of humanitarian aid to all who need it. See Convention (IV) Relative to the Protection of Civilian Persons in Time of War, Geneva, August 12, 1949; Protocol Additional to the Geneva Conventions of 12 August 1949, and relating to the Protection of Victims of International Armed Conflicts (Protocol I), June 8, 1977; and Protocol Additional to the Geneva Conventions of 12 August 1949, and relating to the Protection of Victims of Non-International Armed Conflicts (Protocol II), June 8, 1977. Other principles and laws related to humanitarian assistance are laid out in

Displacement—which occurs when conflict forces people to leave their homes—may create large communities of those needing humanitarian assistance. The displaced include refugees, who flee to other states, and internally displaced persons (IDPs), who seek refuge elsewhere within the country. As the situation stabilizes, provisions must be made for the return or resettlement of these displaced persons according to their preferences and what conditions allow. Rapid returns of the displaced may be destabilizing because returnees may overwhelm fragile social services that are still being rebuilt. Returnees can become involved in property disputes with squatters or others who have moved into their homes.[7]

If the situation does not stabilize, or if return is impossible for substantial numbers of people, longer-term solutions have to be found to ensure that displaced populations do not suffer more than necessary and that their displacement does not contribute to broader security problems. For instance, if large numbers of the displaced are living in camps rather than in rented housing, dangers can arise. Displaced populations can, over time, become susceptible to radicalization, particularly because refugee and IDP camps can become a source of both recruits and supplies (including food) for insurgents. Large refugee populations can spread the conflict to neighboring nations, particularly if the needs of refugees are not effectively met. A lack of access to education for young people will, over time, result in a wide range of long-term damage to a country's security and capacity for development.

Resettlement for those who cannot return is therefore crucial and requires that services are provided and needs met both immediately and in the long term. Resettlement in the location of the initial displacement may be pursued if doing so is sustainable and effective;

International Committee of the Red Cross, "International Humanitarian Law," Web page, undated. An excellent overview of humanitarian law and principles can be found in Field Manual 3-07, *Stability Operations*, Appendix E.

[7] Property disputes are particularly destabilizing in the aftermath of ethnic or sectarian conflicts, when displaced persons from one group frequently return home to find members of another group living in their houses. This is especially problematic if the latter group was involved in ethnic cleansing or other violence that caused the displaced to flee in the first place.

otherwise, it should occur in a different location. Long-term camp or squatter situations must be avoided through efforts with host communities to either integrate the displaced or find new homes for them. Ideally, resettlement should happen in the early stages of the displacement, but this will not always be possible.

Governance

Most stabilization and reconstruction operations occur in areas where national or local authorities are either weak or unable to function. Rebuilding the basic capacity of the state to provide services and administer itself is a high priority in these operations. Doing so usually requires intervening forces to (1) support and assist national authorities in the provision of such services as education, electrical power, and health care and (2) help municipal authorities provide local water, sewer, and trash-collection services. If local authorities have collapsed or been forcibly removed from power, intervening forces may have to temporarily assume the functions of government while simultaneously trying to build new government institutions that can ultimately enable indigenous authorities to resume power.

Building national and local government institutions simultaneously requires a careful balancing act. Many important services are provided at the local level, so building institutions from the bottom up can help ensure that services reach citizens quickly and can empower new political actors who were not part of the previous power structure. Yet, it can be very destabilizing to develop strong local authorities before national authorities because doing so establishes de facto decentralization and can exacerbate sectarian and ethnic conflicts in deeply divided societies.[8]

Economic Stabilization

Economic stabilization involves immediate tasks to help the economy start functioning again. One of the most important tasks is establishing a stable currency to facilitate the resumption of commerce. Economic activity often slows or stops in unstable countries, and currency

---

[8] Dobbins et al., 2007, pp. 135–155.

values can fluctuate wildly. Stabilizing the currency can thus help promote economic growth. It also involves (1) building the capacity of the central government to collect revenue and make expenditures with a minimum of corruption and (2) establishing a legal and regulatory framework that encourages trade and investment.[9]

Development

Once stability is created, longer-term goals can be pursued. A 2007 RAND publication classifies these efforts as lower priorities when resources are constrained.[10] Other analysts argue that economic growth and development can prevent a return to conflict and thus must be considered high priorities.[11] Still others hold that rapid political and economic development benefits groups unevenly, which can foster discontent and lead to political violence.[12] There is no disagreement, however, with the assertion that development facilitates a country's long-term growth and prosperity. Growth and prosperity are critical components of reconstruction efforts. It is worth noting, however, that efforts to advance them may fail if security, humanitarian-assistance, and governance tasks are not successfully resourced and executed. Economies do not thrive in times of conflict.

Development involves promoting economic growth, reducing poverty, and improving infrastructure. Development issues are present in many places around the world that are politically stable, so stabilization and reconstruction operations should not focus directly on these tasks. Instead, their mission should be to stabilize the security situation and build the capacity of the state so that a wide range of develop-

---

[9]   Dobbins et al., 2007, pp. 161–178. See also the discussion in Ashraf Ghani and Clare Lockhart, *Fixing Failed States: A Framework for Rebuilding a Fractured World*, Oxford, UK: Oxford University Press, 2008, pp. 135–139.

[10]   Dobbins et al., 2007, pp. 13–15.

[11]   The discussion in U.S. Agency for International Development, *A Guide to Economic Growth in Post-Conflict Countries*, Washington, D.C., 2008, cites the work of Paul Collier to make this argument.

[12]   Samuel P. Huntington, *Political Order in Changing Societies,* New Haven, Conn.: Yale University Press, 1968, pp. 39–56.

ment actors—including the World Bank, specialized UN agencies, and NGOs—can work with the government to develop and execute effective development programs. Similarly, intervening forces should invest in emergency repairs to infrastructure and leave longer-term infrastructure investments to international financial institutions or the private sector.[13]

Deployed military and civilian personnel are economic actors in their own right, and their efforts have an impact on political and economic development goals. They should be aware of the principles of oversight, accountability, respect for human rights, and civilian control, each of which should be integrated into all stabilization and reconstruction efforts. Moreover, military and civilian personnel must be aware of the impact that their local hiring practices, land rental, use of transportation, and other actions have on the local economy and take care that their presence does not create dangerous distortions. All personnel should carefully avoid favoritism based on sex or ethnicity in determining to whom they award contracts and ensure that transparency and accountability, to the extent possible, drive their approaches to reconstruction.

Democratization

U.S. efforts to assist in the political reconstruction of other countries, whether following conflict or under other circumstances, traditionally contain a strong element of democratization. Democratization generally refers to the transition to and development of a liberal democratic system of government that (1) assures civil liberties for the public, consistent free and fair elections, and a free press and (2) establishes checks and balances, accountability to the public, a strong civil society, and respect for the broad range of human rights. Inherent in this process is a focus on assuring minority rights and the rights of women. This transformational agenda has not been part of many past efforts to stabilize and reconstruct countries. A functional government was generally the goal of such efforts, and civil liberties and rights took a back seat. That

---

[13] Dobbins et al., 2007, pp. 213–241.

said, democratization has long been a factor in official U.S. policy and has been increasingly emphasized in the past couple of decades.

As U.S. experiences in Iraq and Afghanistan show, democratization is both difficult and controversial. Early elections in states where political divides reflect sectarian divisions can deepen splits within the population and retard reconciliation. Efforts to equalize treatment of the formerly underprivileged frustrate and anger the formerly privileged. Conversely, failure to provide advantages to the formerly underprivileged, who see in the intervention an opportunity to gain control over former oppressors, can also cause frustration and anger.

There are both practical and ideological reasons for including democratization in U.S. foreign-assistance projects. These reasons are not unrelated, as those who believe in democracy ideologically tend also to believe in it practically, seeing it as the best possible system. Proponents underscore the better systems and better government that emerge when political leaders are accountable to the people. Corruption and abuse of public funds are less likely when a free press and checks and balances in an elected government are in place. Supporters of democratization argue that greater equality amongst all people creates a more meritocratic state in which the most capable can do that which they are best able to do. From an economic standpoint, at least, there is consistent evidence that equal education and opportunities for people regardless of gender correlate with higher levels of development.[14]

The most common arguments against democratization concern the desire to maintain local traditions and allow countries to find their own ways; or, they claim that the transition to democracy is itself destabilizing. Such arguments can be misused, however, to justify oppressive and corrupt politics that, in the long term, prevent effec-

---

[14] Good overviews of the literature on this issue can be found in Mayra Buvinic and Andrew R. Morrison, "Introduction, Overview, and Future Policy Agenda," in Mayra Buvinic, Andrew R. Morrison, A. Waafas Ofosu-Amaah, and Mirja Sjöblom, eds., *Equality For Women: Where Do We Stand on Equality Development Goal 3?* Washington, D.C.: The International Bank for Reconstruction and Development/The World Bank, 2008, pp. 4–7; and World Bank, "Promoting Gender Equality and Women's Empowerment," in World Bank, *Global Monitoring Report 2007: Millennium Development Goals: Confronting the Challenges of Gender Equality and Fragile States*, Washington, D.C.: World Bank, 2007, pp. 107–111.

tive development. Furthermore, most stabilization and reconstruction operations occur in places where the previous governments have been delegitimized and discredited. Some form of popular sovereignty and representative government may be the only viable option for reestablishing a government that the population will view as legitimate over the long term.

The bottom line is that the promotion of democracy has been a consistent component of U.S. foreign policy for many years and a particular focus since the end of the Cold War. Most future U.S. stabilization and reconstruction interventions will include at least some democratization goals.

It is worth noting that the specific form of democracy may not be terribly important. It does not matter if the country follows a parliamentary or presidential model, for example, as long as the form of government reflects the needs of the particular society and enables citizens to express their views freely and choose representative leaders.[15] A country with a long history of unitary government may resist federal structures, for example, and a country with deep ethnic or sectarian cleavages would be better off with institutional arrangements that promote consensus and compromise rather than a winner-take-all system. Regardless of the specific institutional arrangements, the ideals and goals of democracy ought to permeate all efforts at building government institutions if such efforts are to endure.

Defining Capacity Requirements

The preceding discussion outlined the key components of stabilization and reconstruction. From these components we derive some specific capacity requirements and assess what personnel might be needed and available to carry out these tasks.

---

[15] Dobbins et al., 2007, pp. 189–209.

Policing

It is very unlikely that local civilian police will be capable of restoring law and order. The stabilization operation will therefore need to (1) help achieve initial stability, (2) maintain stability once stability is attained, and (3) assist in the development of local police. These tasks are among the most important missions in the entire operation.

Ideally, a deployable civilian police force with a training capability will be available to take on these tasks as part of the stabilization operation. Current capacity for these tasks in the U.S. government is very limited, however, as discussed in Chapter Three. Some foreign partners have a greater deployable police capacity, but no one country has standing forces of sufficient size to independently carry out large-scale stabilization missions in a foreign country. Although the United Nations is able to deploy civilian police in various contingencies, it relies on short-term hires from member states to support these deployments. These capabilities will be insufficient and will not benefit any operations in which the UN is not directly involved.

Even if deployable civilian police can be brought into a theater, there will likely not be enough of them present at the outset of an operation to take on these tasks, especially in the aftermath of military operations. Military personnel, who can be deployed quickly and easily and may already be in place, will probably be used at the outset, and possibly for longer, even though they are not ideally suited to these tasks.[16]

In the past, military personnel have taken on immediate stabilization tasks and performed them admirably. However, these experiences show that if military personnel are to carry out immediate stabilization tasks, several negative repercussions should be avoided. First, the duties and training of military personnel are fundamentally different from those of police. Use of force, attitudes toward the local population, and detention of suspicious persons are all governed by very different rules for police than they are for the military. Police are generally well-versed in local laws, and their primary mission is to protect the general public. This is not the primary mission of military forces, who are deployed to

---

[16] Dobbins et al., 2007, pp. 24–28.

win a conflict. The use of military approaches and tactics under such circumstances can be counterproductive and dangerous, possibly spurring local opposition. Second, while it is possible to train military personnel in policing approaches, most of the military personnel available for such missions will not have such training to an adequate extent. Third, unless the military presence is especially large, choices will have to be made between the stabilization task and other missions, possibly to the detriment of all. Fourth, the presence of a foreign military force as a longer-term source of security and stability is likely to be viewed by the local population as occupation, a perspective that can further spur opposition. Although this last risk can also accompany a foreign police presence, the impact on the population of using specifically military forces may be substantial.

There is, of course, a category of military personnel with police training: military police (MPs). During the immediate stabilization period, MPs can play an important role in bridging capability gaps, particularly when significant combat operations are still required. However, as a long-term solution, MPs are problematical. Their primary mission is to police the military, not perform civilian policing in a foreign country. While there are more overlaps between these missions than between those of most military forces and police, there are also important disconnects and gaps in training and approach. MPs are not trained to respond to large-scale violence, such as riots, or looting. It would be possible to amend the mission and training of MPs to encompass stabilization and policing abroad, but this would require substantial resources and careful implementation to ensure that the traditional MP mission did not suffer. More importantly, however, doing so would further cement the military playing a role in what is fundamentally a civilian task, which would pose all the associated dangers discussed above.

The situation is even more dire when it comes to training police for community policing or such high-end missions as counterinsurgency and counterterrorism. Military personnel are quite simply not equipped to deliver this training, although they have worked hard to set up effective programs when so tasked (as in Iraq and Afghanistan). As discussed above, although MPs are better suited than most military personnel for this mission, training civilian police in a foreign country is a long way from their core mission and tasks, and they are therefore far from an ideal solution. Efforts to utilize reservists and members of the National Guard who are or have been police officers may be more effective. However, such efforts will disrupt deployments of extant reserve and Guard units and create significant challenges for planning—quite possibly without generating sufficient police to do the job. Furthermore, all use of military personnel to train civilian police could undercut the effort to build truly civilian policing.

The alternative for both law and order missions and police training is the development of deployable civilian police capacity. However, large numbers of readily available, deployable police for long-term operations will almost certainly remain a tall order for some time. Current capabilities and efforts are far from sufficient.

Law and Order

The United States also lacks deployable civilian capacity for other law and order tasks. Although the Department of Justice has expertise in the rule of law, it has less knowledge of foreign legal institutions and systems and few deployable personnel. In some countries, local law prohibits the use of foreign judges and attorneys. Using foreign personnel to dispense justice should be avoided because it weakens trust in the local government and reinforces a feeling of foreign occupation. In some cases, however, there may be no alternative. The same principles also apply to prisons and corrections systems.

As in the case of policing, easily deployed military personnel will not have the capacity to carry out all of these tasks on their own. The U.S. military's military courts differ in many ways from civilian courts and are busy fulfilling their own responsibilities. Integrating the effort to build security institutions into broader governance will require both civilian involvement and integration with broader reconstruction efforts. Stabilization operations will have to seek to leverage what already exists in the country while providing assistance and advice to ensure that processes work and that sufficient courts and prisons are staffed with sufficient and qualified personnel. To assure sustainability and alignment with other goals, assistance providers should incorporate transparency, accountability, and human rights into their efforts to rebuild law, order, and national security. This combination is difficult in a postconflict environment.

The level and mix of required deployable capacity will vary with circumstances but will by definition include specialists (i.e., attorneys and judges) with expertise in a variety of types of law and knowledge of local legal and cultural features. It should also include specialists in corrections. In some cases, a comparatively small number of advisors will be required to advise and assist their local colleagues. In others, large numbers of advisors will be needed to oversee legal procedures and perhaps even carry out certain tasks themselves.

Military and Intelligence Training and Capacity Building

One area in which military personnel may be effectively used is in training the armed forces of the host country. The U.S. military has military trainers and carries out a good bit of training abroad. In the case of intelligence, however, as with law and order, the military is not the ideal trainer (although military intelligence may need to be factored into the development of military capacity). Traditionally, U.S. and allied civilian intelligence agencies have taken the lead in building intelligence capacity in countries where reconstruction efforts are ongoing. In both cases, capacity is either sufficient or can be ramped up.

It is no less important to maintain effective and transparent civilian and political oversight of these efforts and ensure that they are effective, accountable, and integrated into broader security sector and government development goals than it is in other aspects of reconstruction. Inculcating appropriate oversight may involve training host-country government personnel to serve as civilian overseers of military training and operations. It may also require establishing transparent and appropriate oversight of intelligence training and functions.

Disarmament, Demobilization, and Reintegration

Either civilian or military specialists or a combination of both can effectively implement the early disarmament and demobilization components of DDR. They can only do so, however, if such efforts are integrated into and flow from a broader political-reconciliation process. Thus, civilian involvement is critical. The reintegration task will require reintegration specialists who possess relevant expertise about the conflict and the host country and are integrated into the overall development goals for the host country. The U.S. military has limited experience in implementing DDR programs, although some relevant expertise and experience do exist within various U.S. government agencies. The UN, by contrast, has accumulated significant expertise in this area. Working with a range of international actors to leverage this sort of experience can be crucial to ensuring the success of DDR programs.

Humanitarian Assistance

Humanitarian-assistance specialists exist in the U.S. government, international organizations, and the NGO community. Indeed, non-governmental humanitarian relief organizations will likely already be on the ground before most stabilization and reconstruction operations commence, unless widespread violence has forced such organizations to leave the country. In the latter case, U.S. government civilian and military personnel may be required to directly provide humanitarian assistance until the situation is secure enough for the relief organizations to return. In the former case, U.S. government personnel are more likely to be involved in coordinating international and domestic relief actors than in directly providing assistance to individuals.

Some U.S. military personnel know how to support and even implement humanitarian-assistance efforts effectively. However, civilian provision of humanitarian assistance is vastly preferable to military provision. Military personnel are frequently not viewed as honest brokers, and they may be perceived as using humanitarian aid for political goals. Sometimes, combatants assist communities they perceive as allies, or do so in the hope of creating such allies. This is both contrary to the principles of humanitarian-assistance provision and counterproductive to stabilization and reconstruction goals. Military provision of humanitarian assistance should be a last resort implemented only when other options are simply not feasible.

The single most important contribution that U.S. military personnel can make to humanitarian efforts is to ensure a reasonably secure environment that enables relief agencies to operate freely and access needy populations.[17] The military can establish safe corridors for the provision of aid. If humanitarian relief organizations can access some parts of the country but not all areas in need, military personnel may sometimes deliver assistance on behalf of those organizations and groups. This activity, however, should be very carefully managed and coordinated.[18]

Ideally, the U.S. government will not need to deploy large numbers of civilian government personnel to provide humanitarian assistance and will instead be able to rely on nongovernmental and international actors. However, USAID, State, and DoD will have to be involved in planning for humanitarian aid efforts and will need means to communicate and cooperate with a broad range of actors. In some cases, the United States will have to deploy or hire people to implement aid programs. The capacity for these efforts generally exists, but it may prove challenging to mobilize.

Governance, Democratization, and Human Rights

In the immediate aftermath of conflict, U.S. personnel may have to help govern the host country. Over time, they can transition into an advisory role, helping civil servants rebuild government institutions. The knowledge required for these efforts is specialized, and the U.S. military is not well suited for such tasks.[19] All efforts to develop and rebuild governance should be coordinated and aligned with the longer-term goals and needs of the host country.

---

[17] Dobbins et al., 2007 pp. 109–134. See also Crane et al., 2009.

[18] In cases when it is otherwise impossible to deliver assistance, the military can, for example, carry out air drops of food aid. Although this is a highly inefficient means of delivery, it can be better than nothing.

[19] Although military personnel have done well in implementing these tasks, this is more a testament to these individuals than to the advisability of using of military forces for such tasks.

Expertise and knowledge about how to effectively manage and rebuild national and local capacity exists within the United States, but not in a large and readily deployable form. Instead, this capacity is spread throughout the U.S. government (particularly USAID and the State Department), analytical community, and advocacy community. Both practical expertise and willingness to deploy (and government capacity to organize such personnel for deployment) may be difficult to secure. Expertise also resides in IOs and NGOs worldwide, but U.S. willingness to outsource these efforts will depend on the specifics of the operation.

Economic Stabilization and Development

Economic experts will be needed both to restart the economy and guide development. As with broader governance goals, military roles in this sector are limited, and demand for qualified civilian advisors to take part in reconstruction efforts is high.

Expertise for these tasks exists in USAID and State, but the ability to deploy it in sufficient numbers is questionable. Other agencies may also have relevant expertise, but this is an issue to approach carefully. Knowing the workings of financial markets or agriculture in the United States does not always translate into an understanding of how these systems work elsewhere. Expertise also exists in the IO and NGO communities, which can be leveraged in many cases, and in the academic community, which can be leveraged if circumstances permit. Fundamentally, many of the same issues seen in the case of political development also accompany economic stabilization and development.

Developing Capacity

Recent years have seen significant effort on the part of the U.S. government to expand both its own capacity and its ability to leverage skills found elsewhere. While these efforts have sometimes lacked coherence, they demonstrate the U.S. government's recognition that gaps exist. The next chapter describes recent efforts to improve U.S. capacity for stabilization and reconstruction operations and identifies the main challenges that remain to be addressed.

CHAPTER THREE

Recent Efforts to Build Capacity

In the past few years, the U.S. government has undertaken a number of important initiatives to build capacity for stabilization and reconstruction operations. This chapter provides a brief overview of these efforts, starting with the creation of the Office of the Coordinator for Reconstruction and Stabilization (S/CRS) within the State Department and related presidential directives and legislation. It then briefly describes two S/CRS concepts for how the U.S. government should plan and conduct stabilization and reconstruction operations. Next, it discusses the current state of U.S. government deployable civilian capacity, including development of the Civilian Response Corps. The chapter concludes by describing some of the remaining challenges related to interagency operations and stabilization and reconstruction.

The Office of the Coordinator for Reconstruction and Stabilization: Creation, Interagency Direction, and Legislation

The Creation of S/CRS

In the aftermath of the invasion of Iraq, it became clear that the United States needed to improve its ability to coordinate the various civilian aspects of stabilization and reconstruction. In early 2004, the Senate and then the House introduced legislation that would have directed the Secretary of State to stand up an Office for International Stabilization and Reconstruction in the State Department. The Secretary of

State preempted the congressional legislation by creating S/CRS in July 2004. The office's stated mission is to

> lead, coordinate, and institutionalize U.S. Government civilian capacity to prevent or prepare for post-conflict situations, and to help stabilize and reconstruct societies in transition from conflict or civil strife so they can reach a sustainable path towards peace, democracy and a market economy.[1]

Ambassador Carlos Pascual served as the first coordinator; he was succeeded by Ambassador John Herbst in March 2006.

One of S/CRS's first tasks was developing and negotiating National Security Presidential Directive (NSPD)-44, *Management of Interagency Efforts Concerning Reconstruction and Stabilization*,[2] the directive that codified the office's role in the interagency approach to stabilization and reconstruction operations. The process of negotiating NSPD-44 underlined the challenges inherent in S/CRS's role. The office had to build interagency buy-in for its leadership of future efforts. Many senior DoD officials, including those at the very highest levels, saw the new organization in a positive light, hoping that it would coordinate and build civilian capacity and take some unwanted load from DoD. Many key actors in the State Department and USAID, however, were more suspicious, believing that S/CRS was seeking to take over functions that were traditionally their own. S/CRS staff, for their part, saw the new entity as one created to reform entrenched State Department and USAID bureaucracies that had failed in Afghanistan and Iraq. They believed that key actors in State and USAID were seeking to sideline the new office to maintain the status quo. Relations were tense throughout the negotiation process. After NSPD-44 was signed in December 2005, giving S/CRS greater legitimacy, the office's leadership took steps to build bridges with other offices in the State Department and USAID in order to begin implementing NSPD-44.

---

[1]   Nora Bensahel, "Organising for Nation Building," *Survival*, Vol. 49, No. 2, Summer 2007, p. 44.

[2]   The White House, National Security Presidential Directive/NSPD-44, *Management of Interagency Efforts Concerning Reconstruction and Stabilization*, December 7, 2005.

NSPD-44, S/CRS, and Interagency Roles

NSPD-44 gave the Secretary of State responsibility for coordinating and leading U.S. government efforts to plan, prepare, and conduct stabilization and reconstruction operations. S/CRS is the lead office for fulfilling the Secretary of State's responsibilities under NSPD-44.

Technically, NSPD-44 superseded Presidential Decision Directive (PDD)-56, *Managing Complex Contingency Operations*,[3] which was adopted by the Clinton administration in May 1997. However, the two documents served different purposes. PDD-56 was designed to codify interagency lessons learned in complex contingency operations, while NSPD-44 focuses more on the roles and responsibilities of the State Department and S/CRS. Furthermore, PDD-56 effectively lapsed at the end of the Clinton administration, and the G. W. Bush administration did not adopt policy guidance in this area until NSPD-44.[4]

Among other things, NSPD-44 created the standing Policy Coordinating Committee (PCC) for Reconstruction and Stabilization Operations.[5] S/CRS cochairs the PCC with the National Security Council (NSC) Senior Director for Stability Operations. In addition, S/CRS staff chair a number of sub-PCCs. The sub-PCCs include all departments and agencies involved in stabilization and reconstruction, but in practice, DoD, State, and USAID are the main players. This makes sense because these organizations control the majority of relevant capabilities.[6] S/CRS is at the center of interagency-coordination

---

[3] The White House, Presidential Decision Directive/PDD-56, *Managing Complex Contingency Operations*, May 1997.

[4] The G. W. Bush administration did draft policy guidance in this area early in its first term, but it remained unsigned and never went into effect. See Michèle Flournoy, "Interagency Strategy and Planning for Post-Conflict Reconstruction," in Robert C. Orr, ed., *Winning the Peace: An American Strategy for Post-Conflict Reconstruction*, Washington, D.C.: Center for Strategic and International Studies, 2004, especially pp. 107–108.

[5] The NSC also created a Senior Director for Relief, Stabilization, and Development, later renamed Senior Director for Stability Operations. However, this position was not created specifically in response to NSPD-44.

[6] Thomas S. Szayna, Derek Eaton, James E. Barnett II, Brooke Stearns Lawson, Terrence K. Kelly, and Zachary Haldeman, *Integrating Civilian Agencies in Stability Operations*, Santa Monica, Calif.: RAND Corporation, MG-801-A, forthcoming.

processes for stabilization, reconstruction, and implementation of NSPD-44. Below, we list some of the key initiatives of NSPD-44 and assess the progress of each.

Develop strategies and ensure policy and program coordination for foreign assistance related to stabilization and reconstruction. Foreign assistance for stabilization and reconstruction has been tied to the larger issue of foreign-assistance reform at the State Department. In January 2006, the Secretary of State established the position of Director of U.S. Foreign Assistance "to better align our foreign assistance programs with our foreign policy goals."[7] Despite the modest title, the director reports directly to the Secretary and is also double-hatted as the director of USAID. In October 2006, the director approved the first Foreign Assistance Framework, which aligned foreign-policy goals with different country categories. One of these categories was "rebuilding countries," defined as "states in or emerging from and rebuilding after internal or external conflict."[8] S/CRS and the Director of Foreign Assistance cooperate closely on foreign assistance for this country category.

Lead interagency planning to prevent or mitigate conflict. S/CRS has conducted interagency planning for operations in Sudan, Haiti, Kosovo, and Afghanistan, but it has not always been in the lead. S/CRS has generally carried out its planning efforts in support of the relevant State Department regional bureau or the chief of mission (COM). This may not have been the original intent of NSPD-44, but it has been effective. The State Department regional bureaus and the COMs retain responsibility for implementation and continue to play the lead role, both in Washington, D.C., and in the field, in developing and implementing broader policy related to the countries in question.[9]

---

[7]   Secretary of State Condoleezza Rice, "Remarks on Foreign Assistance," January 19, 2006.

[8]   U.S. Department of State, *Foreign Assistance Framework*, July 10, 2007.

[9]   In Washington, D.C., the NSC regional staff is generally small and relies heavily on State Department regional bureaus, which are larger. In the G. W. Bush administration, the regional Assistant Secretary of State was a key player in regional PCCs. In the field, the COM has, in almost all cases, authority over all U.S. activities in a country. She or he runs

The distinction between lead and support may not matter as much now as it did when S/CRS was first stood up. In fact, related NSPD-44 language may have been counterproductive. It alienated the State Department regional bureaus that could have helped with coordination both internally within the State Department and externally in the interagency community. The regional bureaus worried that S/CRS would take responsibility for overall policy toward key countries away from them. When this did not happen, regional bureaus began to recognize the added value (including additional personnel) S/CRS could bring to some of their most difficult problems.

S/CRS's first attempt to coordinate interagency planning met with mixed results. In 2005, the Secretary of State asked S/CRS to help address the evolving crisis in Sudan. S/CRS's first step was to set up a Country Reconstruction and Stabilization Group (CRSG), which was, essentially, a PCC. It was clear that this decision was not well coordinated with the State Department's regional bureau or the existing Africa PCC, which had been meeting to discuss Sudan for months. S/CRS eventually abandoned the Sudan CRSG and merged its efforts with the Africa PCC. Subsequent planning efforts fared better, in large part because S/CRS conducted them in support of the State Department's relevant regional bureau. In 2006, for example, S/CRS helped the Bureau of Western Hemisphere Affairs develop a one-year strategic plan for Haiti, which led to the Haiti Stabilization Initiative. S/CRS's most comprehensive planning effort supported the Bureau of European and Eurasian Affairs. S/CRS helped develop a medium-term strategic plan for the four years following Kosovo's independence. S/CRS recently sent an eight-person planning team to Afghanistan in support of the Bureau of Near Eastern Affairs and the U.S. embassy in Kabul.

Each of these efforts has provided insights into how to plan for stabilization and reconstruction operations. These insights informed the development of a planning framework that we describe below. However, these deployments have also consumed the attention of S/CRS's

---

the country team, which includes representatives from all departments and agencies represented in the country.

planning staff, leaving the office little time to develop contingency plans or think strategically about prioritizing countries for planning.

Identify states at risk of instability. S/CRS works with the National Intelligence Council to develop the Internal Instability Watchlist, a classified intelligence product that is updated semi-annually. It lists countries in order of their likelihood of failure over the next six months.

Although NSPD-44 specifically tasks S/CRS only with identifying states at risk of instability, the logical next step is to prioritize these states in terms of U.S. national security interests. One common way to prioritize contingencies is by evaluating their likelihood and consequence. For example, the use of nuclear weapons against the United States is generally considered to be low likelihood and high consequence. Establishing clear priorities can help with contingency-planning efforts and capability development.[10]

Develop detailed contingency plans for reconstruction and stabilization scenarios and integrate them with military plans. S/CRS has not developed plans for any future contingencies, with one partial exception. When the State Department assumed leadership of the Commission for Assistance to a Free Cuba (CAFC) in December 2005, S/CRS took the lead for interagency planning. However, this was not a new planning effort: CAFC had been conducting interagency planning since it was first established in October 2003. S/CRS intends to develop interagency plans for future contingencies, but no such efforts have been started as of this writing.

---

[10] Both the DoD and the Department of Homeland Security (DHS) maintain lists of contingencies and scenarios for exactly these reasons. Title 10 requires the Secretary of Defense to develop a prioritized list of contingency plans for approval by the President. This list is currently part of the *Guidance for Employment of the Force* and was previously part of the *Contingency Planning Guidance*. The Department of Homeland Security is using the National Planning Scenarios to guide contingency planning under White House, Homeland Security Presidential Directive/HSPD-8, *National Preparedness*, December 17, 2003, Annex I.

The Reconstruction and Stabilization Civilian Management Act of 2008

On October 14, 2008, the President signed into law the Reconstruction and Stabilization Civilian Management Act of 2008.[11] This act formally establishes the S/CRS at the State Department. Previously, the Secretary of State appointed the coordinator; under the new act, the President appoints the coordinator with the advice and consent of the Senate. The coordinator will continue to report directly to the Secretary of State.

The act provides the necessary authority to develop the Response Readiness Corps (composed of active and standby components, discussed below) and the Civilian Reserve Corps. It adds an important caveat to the Civilian Reserve Corps, however, stating that the Corps should "avoid substantially impairing the capacity and readiness of State and local governments from which Civilian Reserve Corps personnel may be drawn."[12]

The act also provides the Secretary of State with new personnel authorities, such as extending benefit coverage, that will make it easier to deploy civilians in conflict environments. It also gives the President the authority to reprogram funds to assist in stabilizing or reconstructing a country. However, this authority is severely limited: The President cannot transfer funds between accounts or departments. Essentially, this means that within a funding account, the President can transfer funds from one country to another. In addition to providing new authorities, the act also includes two requirements: The Secretary of State must develop (1) an interagency strategy to respond to stabilization and reconstruction operations, including a plan to coordinate the U.S. government activities, and (2) an annual report to Congress on implementation of the act.

---

[11] Public Law 110-417, Title XVI, The Reconstruction and Stabilization Civilian Management Act of 2008, July 14, 2008. The act is sometimes called "Lugar-Biden" after the last names of its two original sponsors. The bill was first introduced in the Senate in February 2004.

[12] Public Law 110-417, Title XVI, The Reconstruction and Stabilization Civilian Management Act of 2008.

S/CRS Concepts for Planning and Conducting Operations

In addition to the initiatives discussed above, S/CRS has also developed two concepts for how the U.S. government should plan and conduct stabilization and reconstruction operations: the *Planning Framework for Reconstruction, Stabilization and Conflict Transformation*, and the Interagency Management System for Reconstruction and Stabilization (which has three subcomponents). These two concepts build on lessons identified from recent stabilization and reconstruction operations.

The *Planning Framework for Reconstruction, Stabilization and Conflict Transformation*

The purpose of the *Planning Framework for Reconstruction, Stabilization and Conflict Transformation* is to provide a guide for how the U.S. government should develop civilian plans for stabilization and reconstruction operations. The document was authored primarily by S/CRS, with significant assistance from DoD. The first draft of the framework was sent out for interagency comment in December 2005, near the time NSPD-44 was signed. Comments were so plentiful that efforts to revise the document faltered until early 2008. Rather than rewrite the framework in response to the comments, S/CRS decided to draft a much shorter document outlining the principles of the Planning Framework. The Reconstruction and Stabilization PCC approved this shorter document in May 2008.

The principles document outlines two broad types of interagency planning: crisis-response planning and long-term, scenario-based planning. Crisis-response planning addresses an imminent or existing crisis. Long-term, scenario-based planning addresses potential future crises, usually years in advance. In this respect, long-term planning is similar to the military's contingency or deliberate planning.

The principles document also outlines a planning process consisting of four steps: situation analysis, policy formulation, strategy development, and interagency implementation planning. Situation analysis is most useful for analyzing an imminent or existing crisis to gather information and building an accurate picture of conditions and developments. The goal of the policy-formulation step is to get planning guidance, including the overall goal of the operation and any critical planning assumptions or considerations that need to be factored into the plan, from senior leaders in the Deputies Committee or Principals Committee.[13] Strategy development and interagency implementation planning are the two phases of plan development. Development of the strategic plan occurs in Washington at the PCC level, and development of the implementation plan occurs within the country team.

One of the primary challenges in reaching interagency agreement on the principles document lay in the difficulties of reconciling military and civilian planning cultures.[14] DoD and the State Department have very different approaches to planning, in large part because of their different missions. S/CRS initially shared the State Department's planning culture, which focuses on programmatic planning for the next fiscal year (FY) and not on planning for unforeseen contingencies. Over time, however, the office's specific mission led it to adopt more contingency-planning approaches in support of its long-term, scenario-based planning.

The planning framework has been used to help develop plans for ongoing operations in Haiti, Kosovo, and Afghanistan. It has not yet been used to develop a contingency plan that can be integrated with existing military plans.

The Interagency Management System

S/CRS began work on the Interagency Management System (IMS) while it was still negotiating NSPD-44. The IMS is a concept for how the U.S. government would operate during a stabilization and reconstruction scenario. In March 2007, the Deputies Committee approved the overall IMS concept. There is still much work to be done to turn the IMS concept into a reality, however. The IMS has three main components—a policy coordination group, a civilian planning cell, and deployable civilian teams—which we describe below.

---

[13] These committees are interagency forums in which policies and issues related to national security are discussed. The Principals Committee meets at the cabinet level, while the Deputies Committee meets at the subcabinet level.

[14] For a fuller discussion see Szayna et al., forthcoming.

The Country Reconstruction and Stabilization Group. The CRSG is best described as a PCC with a dedicated secretariat responsible for managing a crisis. It is not a standing body and is formed only in response to a crisis. The CRSG can be created as a new PCC or be crafted out of an existing PCC (which would be given additional responsibilities). The CRSG is cochaired by the Regional Assistant Secretary, the Coordinator for Reconstruction and Stabilization, and the relevant NSC senior director. The Director of Foreign Assistance leads efforts related to foreign assistance.

The trichair concept was an inelegant compromise reached during negotiations over the IMS. It is more a reflection of internal State Department politics than representative of the best possible strategic-level crisis-management structure. Although the original concept was that the CRSG should be a new PCC, it makes more sense for S/CRS to augment the existing regional PCC leadership structure during a crisis than to try and replace it midstream. As discussed earlier, the creation of a new CRSG for Sudan with a separate leadership structure led to unnecessary duplication, and the CRSG was subsequently merged with the existing regional PCC.

The idea of setting up an interagency group to deal with a crisis is not new. The CRSG concept is in fact similar to the Executive Committee concept in PDD-56. What is new is the idea of having a dedicated secretariat—a concept that may have evolved from the experiences of the interagency working groups for Iraq and Afghanistan. The secretariat reports to the CRSG and is managed by both a policy director from the State Department's regional bureau and a chief operations officer from S/CRS.

The secretariat is not a standing organization; like the CRSG, it is formed during a crisis. As a result, the primary problem associated with the secretariat is staffing, although myriad logistical issues (from office space to email) must also be addressed before the crisis occurs. For example, when the Afghanistan Interagency Working Group was set up at the State Department, members from DoD could not access their email, which significantly lowered their productivity. Such decisions as whether to collocate will depend on the situation and the amount of preparatory work that has been done.

Staffing the secretariat will always pose problems because no department has "extra" policy staff. During a crisis, the same people must simply work longer hours. The success of the secretariat concept will hinge on S/CRS's ability to support the secretariat with additional staff during a crisis and establish mechanisms that help avoid logistical problems that can lower staff productivity.

The Integration Planning Cell. The Integration Planning Cell (IPC) is a group of civilian planners who can be deployed to a COCOM or equivalent multinational headquarters to help integrate civilian and military planning. The IPC does not develop any plans itself. In a crisis, the CRSG secretariat is responsible for developing a strategic plan and the COM is responsible for developing an interagency implementation plan with support from the Advance Civilian Team (ACT).

The IPC is a new concept and is still untested. Its mission is to integrate civilian and military planning for a particular crisis or for an unforeseen contingency. As noted earlier, S/CRS has yet to develop a civilian contingency plan. Without such a plan, the IPC has nothing to integrate with military contingency plans.

Deliberate planning before a crisis is essential to developing a habitual relationship between civilian and military planners. Again, staffing is an issue. There are few civilian planners in the U.S. government,[15] and even fewer have actually put together a contingency plan (as opposed to a plan for an ongoing crisis). In most civilian departments, day-to-day work, which includes myriad small and large "crises," takes priority over preparing for a potential contingency. It remains to be seen whether the IPC will be able to serve as an effective bridge between the civilian and military planning cultures.[16]

Advance Civilian Teams and Field Advance Civilian Teams. An ACT consists of interagency staff that can be deployed into a country during a crisis to coordinate U.S. stabilization and reconstruction activities. The team operates under COM authority and can either sup-

---

[15] For example, S/CRS's planning office has 30 people, 15–20 of whom are planners. The other employees are administrators, managers, interns, fellows, or subject-matter experts.

[16] For more on the challenges presented by differing military and civilian cultures, see Szayna et al., forthcoming.

plement an existing U.S. embassy or operate without one if none exists. It can also supplement the host government, if one exists.

The Field Advance Civilian Teams (FACTs) are similar to the Provincial Reconstruction Teams (PRTs) deployed in Afghanistan and Iraq. The key difference is that FACTs consist of civilians only, whereas PRT staff are a mix of civilian and military personnel. Part of the rationale for civilian-only teams is that such teams can be deployed with or without U.S. military personnel. For example, ACTs and FACTs could be deployed in support of a UN peacekeeping mission without U.S. military participation.

When U.S. military forces are present, ACTs and FACTs would mirror the military command structure, including the areas of operation. Where possible, the teams would be collocated with counterpart military units and would exchange liaison officers with those units. When the teams must operate in an insecure environment, it is hard to imagine that they would not require additional military staff beyond liaison officers, especially to provide security.

The primary issue with the ACTs and FACTs is staffing. Implementation of the Coalition Provisional Authority (CPA) in Iraq and PRTs in Afghanistan and Iraq provides a good preview of some of the issues involved. Anecdotal evidence suggests that the CPA was never fully staffed and that the personnel who did volunteer did not always have the necessary skills or experience.[17] Getting enough civilian staffing for PRTs has been notoriously difficult, and many PRTs are therefore heavily staffed with military personnel.

Efforts to Develop Civilian Capacity

The Civilian Response Corps is by far the most ambitious effort to build a deployable civilian capacity. An important related initiative is the National Security Professional Development Program, which is meant to help prepare U.S. government civilians for interagency mis-

---

[17] Terrence K. Kelly, Ellen E. Tunstall, Thomas S. Szayna, and Deanna Weber Prine, *Stabilization and Reconstruction Staffing: Developing U.S. Civilian Personnel Capabilities*, Santa Monica, Calif.: RAND Corporation, MG-580-RC, 2008.

sions. In addition, both USAID and DoD have the ability to deploy civilians. USAID regularly deploys small teams to disasters to coordinate U.S. government assistance, and DoD recently announced an effort to improve its ability to deploy civilians.

S/CRS's Civilian Response Corps

The idea of a Civilian Response Corps was originally proposed within the U.S. government by DoD during negotiations pertaining to NSPD-44. S/CRS began studying the idea of a civilian response corps in 2005,[18] and the G. W. Bush administration first requested funding from Congress to begin developing a civilian reserve in its FY07 budget. The initial concept proposed by the military was an institution not dissimilar to the military reserves. As the idea evolved, however, the model diverged from this concept.

The current plan for the Civilian Response Corps includes three components:

- an *active* component composed of 250 full-time U.S. government personnel from eight departments and agencies[19] who are available to deploy within 48 hours. As of this writing, S/CRS had eight active-component personnel who have deployed to Sudan, Chad, Lebanon, Kosovo, Haiti, Afghanistan, and Iraq.
- a *standby* component composed of 2,000 personnel from the same eight agencies who would receive stabilization and reconstruction training and be deployable within 30 days for up to six months
- a *reserve* component composed of 2,000 personnel from the private sector and state and local governments who have unique skills not found in the federal government.

---

[18] Two key studies that have informed debate are Scott Feil et al., *Joint Interagency Evaluation: Civil Reconstruction and Stabilization Reaction Force*, Washington, D.C.: Institute for Defense Analysis, August 2006; and BearingPoint, *Management Study for Establishing a Civilian Reserve*, May 2006.

[19] These eight departments are the Department of State, USAID, the Department of Agriculture, the Department of Commerce, the Department of Health and Human Services, DHS, the Department of Justice, and the Department of the Treasury. See U.S. Department of State, "Fact Sheet: The Civilian Response Corps of the United States of America," July 16, 2008.

The biggest problem associated with implementing the Civilian Response Corps is that Congress has only recently begun to allocate the funds needed to make the corps fully operational. As previously noted, President G. W. Bush first requested funding to begin developing a civilian response corps in his FY07 budget, but Congress rejected this request (in part because it was linked to the Conflict Response Fund).[20] The following year, Congress appropriated $75 million for S/CRS in the 2008 Supplemental Appropriations Act.[21] This funding will enable the office to hire 100 personnel for the active component and 500 for the standby component.[22] The President's FY09 budget request for the Civilian Stabilization Initiative (see Table 3.1) would fully fund the planned Civilian Response Corps.

The Civilian Stabilization Initiative is part of the Department of State, Foreign Operations, and Related Appropriation Act,[23] which has been introduced in the Senate but not yet voted on as of this writing. The current legislation would appropriate $115 million for the Civilian Stabilization Initiative, less than half of the President's request. In addition, it would require the Secretary of State to clarify

> in writing to the Committees on Appropriations the relationship between existing international disaster response capabilities of the United States Government and funding sources (including under the headings "International Disaster Assistance" and "Transition Initiatives" in this Act) and the Civilian Stabilization Initiative.[24]

---

[20] The Conflict Response Fund has been unpopular with Congress. In general, Congress does not allocate funding "just in case" of a crisis. Crises are generally funded through supplemental budgets, which allow greater Congressional oversight. In addition, USAID has two just-in-case funding sources—International Disaster and Famine Assistance and Transition Initiatives—whose existence calls into question the need for a new Conflict Response Fund.

[21] Public Law 110-252, Supplemental Appropriations Act, 2008, June 30, 2008.

[22] Funds must be obligated by September 30, 2009.

[23] U.S. Senate, S.3288, Department of State, Foreign Operations, and Related Programs Appropriations Act, 2009, July 18, 2008.

[24] U.S. Senate, S.3288, Department of State, Foreign Operations, and Related Programs Appropriations Act, 2009.

Table 3.1
FY09 Budget Request for the Civilian Response Corps

Account	FY08—Actual (thousands)	FY09—Request (thousands)
Civilian Stabilization Initiative		
Active and Standby Response Corps	$0	$75,220
U.S. Civilian Reserve Corps	$0	$86,768
Civilian Force Protection, Support and Deployment	$0	$63,629
S/CRS	$7,505	$23,014
Total	$7,505	$248,631

SOURCE: U.S. Department of State, *Summary and Highlights: International Affairs Function 150, Fiscal Year 2009 Budget Request*, undated.

National Security Professional Development

The National Security Professional Development Program has the potential to improve the ability of U.S. government personnel to address a range of interagency issues, including those related to stabilization and reconstruction. It combines several personnel-related initiatives to encourage "jointness" among U.S. government personnel from different departments and agencies. DHS and DoD were early proponents.

The President signed Executive Order 13434, *National Security Professional Development*, in May 2007.[25] The order directed staff from the Homeland and National Security Councils to (1) develop a strategy[26] for putting the National Security Professional Development Program idea into action and (2) set up an executive steering committee.[27]

---

[25] Executive Order 13434, *National Security Professional Development*, May 17, 2007.

[26] The President approved the *National Strategy for the Development of National Security Professionals* in July 2007.

[27] The Director of the Office for Personnel Management chairs the Executive Steering Committee. Other members include the Secretaries of State, Treasury, Defense, Agriculture, Labor, Health and Human Services, Housing and Urban Development, Transportation, Energy, Education, Homeland Security, the Attorney General, the Director of National Intelligence, and the Director of the Office of Management and Budget.

The executive steering committee subsequently set up an integration office and approved an implementation plan.[28] The current governance framework is depicted in Figure 3.1.

Implementation of the National Security Professional Development Program is organized around three pillars: education, training, and professional experience. It can be compared to efforts to achieve jointness in the military spurred by Goldwater-Nichols. The requirement that military personnel serve in a joint duty assignment before they can be promoted to a general or flag-officer grade was one of the

Figure 3.1
National Security Professional Development Program Governance Framework

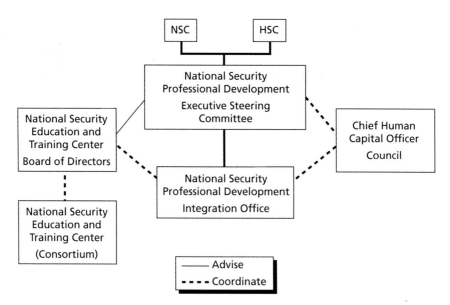

SOURCE: Executive Order 13434, *National Security Professional Development*, May 17, 2007.
NOTE: The board of directors has been established, but the consortium is still under development.
RAND *MG852-3.1*

---

[28] The executive steering committee approved the *National Security Professional Development Implementation Plan* and submitted it to the National and Homeland Security Councils in August 2008.

most lasting legacies of Goldwater-Nichols. The concept of building jointness through assignments to other agencies is similarly incorporated into the National Security Professional Development Program. The strategy includes "Link[ing] career advancement or other incentives for national security professionals to participation in available rotational or temporary detail assignments" as one of the tasks under "professional experience."[29]

Despite the parallels, the implementation plan's requirement for such "professional experience" is not nearly as far-reaching as Goldwater-Nichols's requirement for joint duty assignments. For example, Goldwater-Nichols specifies that assignments within an officer's own military department would not count as a joint duty assignment and that a joint duty assignment would last no less than three years.[30] The *National Strategy for the Development of Security Professionals*, however, cites the following as an example of professional experience: "a temporary detail to another agency, an intra-agency detail within a department, or participating in a relevant interagency working group . . . . [T]hese will normally be of a less than a six-month duration."[31]

Another key issue, and one that is not explicitly addressed in the National Security Professional Development Program, is the different organizational cultures of civilian and military departments and agencies when it comes to education and training. The military tends to *develop* people and civilian departments; agencies tend to *hire* people. These trends are a result of the organizations' different missions. The military focuses on developing people in part because the skill sets required are not easily found in the private sector. The military has a built-in training float,[32] which allows it to devote a large percentage of

---

[29] National Security Professional Development, *National Strategy for the Development of Security Professionals*, July 2007.

[30] Specifically, three years for general and flag officers and three and a half years for other officers. See Public Law 99-433, Title IV, Section 664, Length of Joint Duty Assignments, October 6, 1986.

[31] National Security Professional Development, July 2007.

[32] Essentially, having a training float means that a percentage of personnel billets are set aside for training and education.

personnel time to training, educating, and exercising. Civilian departments and agencies generally do not have a training float, or have only a very small one. In general, these organizations focus on hiring people with existing skill sets; they then provide these employees with on-the-job training and supplemental education and training opportunities. This means that when civilians leave the office to pursue an education or training course, there is often no one available to backfill them. This staffing problem is something that the National Security Professional Development Program will have to address. It is far from insurmountable, however. Various agencies, including the State Department, actually do provide for substantial training and development of their staff.

At present, implementation of the National Security Professional Development Program, now under the direction of the Office of Personnel Management (OPM), has lagged. It could be reenergized with high-level attention, however.

Civilian Capacity at USAID

USAID is one of the few organizations with a long history of rapidly deploying civilians. It can deploy Disaster Assistance Response Teams (DARTs) and Urban Search and Rescue (USAR) Teams within hours of a disaster and initiate transitional development programs within 72 hours of the designation of a crisis. OFDA, located in the Bureau of Democracy, Conflict, and Humanitarian Assistance (DCHA) maintains DARTs and USAR Teams. The Office of Transition Initiatives (OTI), also in DCHA, controls funding for transitional development programs. OFDA's mission is to coordinate U.S. disaster assistance in order to save lives and alleviate immediate human suffering; OTI focuses on providing rapid development assistance that helps set the conditions for long-term development.

DARTs are staffed either by existing USAID personnel or through a program called Response Alternatives for Technical Services, whose participants agree to be hired on a part-time basis (i.e., no more than 130 days per year) and be deployed within hours.[33] USAR Teams are maintained through an agreement with local governments. In exchange

---

[33] Scott Feil et al., 2006.

for additional funding, the fire and rescue departments of Fairfax, Virginia, and Miami-Dade County in Florida agreed to make their teams available for deployments abroad.[34] The policies and procedures for DARTs and USAR Teams are based on the Incident Command System, which is also used during domestic emergency response.

OTI's transitional development programs are very useful for stabilization and reconstruction operations. They fill the gap between immediate humanitarian assistance and long-term development. In fact, the difference between OTI's transitional initiatives program funding and the reconstruction and stabilization program funding requested by S/CRS is unclear. As noted earlier, in the current legislation for the Civilian Stabilization Initiative, Congress requests a written explanation on this point.

In addition to managing the capabilities described above, USAID is increasing its ability to engage with the military. In 2005, USAID created an Office of Military Affairs (OMA), also in DCHA. The primary role of OMA is to provide a focal point for USAID interactions with U.S. and foreign militaries.[35] The creation of OMA has strengthened the relationship between defense and development, a relationship critical for stabilization and reconstruction operations. OMA intends to put a USAID advisor at every COCOM, and many are already in place. It has also placed a senior development advisor at the Pentagon to work with leaders in the Office of the Secretary of Defense and the Joint Staff.

Department of Defense Expeditionary Civilians

The military is not the ideal tool for reconstruction and stabilization operations. However, because it can surge personnel and resources quickly, and because military personnel are already in theater, the Pentagon has taken a leading role in stabilization and reconstruction efforts in Iraq and Afghanistan. DoD recognizes that unless civilians have the capacity to lead stabilization and reconstruction operations, the military will be the fallback option. As a result, it has pursued a

---

[34] The Federal Emergency Management Agency adopted a similar approach to developing USAR Teams for domestic disasters.

[35] USAID published a civilian-military cooperation policy in 2008.

two-pronged strategy. First, it has advocated building civilian capacity at the State Department and USAID. It has also sought to develop its own capabilities, both to ensure readiness to support civilian agencies in stabilization and reconstruction operations and to develop the ability to lead such operations if no one else can do so. As Secretary of Defense Robert Gates has said, "the Armed Forces will need to institutionalize and retain these non-traditional capabilities. . . . But it is no replacement for the real thing—civilian involvement and expertise."[36]

The military has gone a long way toward institutionalizing its ability to support stabilization and reconstruction operations. However, the role DoD civilians play in stabilization and reconstruction operations is often overlooked. DoD has deployed thousands of civilians to Iraq and Afghanistan, but until recently, it has done so in an ad hoc manner. DoD is attempting to institutionalize its process for managing deployable civilians. It recently announced that it intends to build a cadre of expeditionary civilians and track civilian-workforce readiness in a manner similar to the way it tracks the readiness of military forces.[37] These expeditionary civilians would support the full range of DoD's missions, including stabilization and reconstruction.

While it is admirable that DoD wants to better manage its deployable civilians, it remains to be seen whether this proposal will complement other U.S. government efforts, such as the Civilian Response Corps and the National Security Professional Development Program. The Deputy Under Secretary of Defense for Civilian Personnel Policy (DUSD(CPP)) has reportedly expressed a desire to expand the civilian expeditionary corps concept into the interagency community.[38] However, the idea of building an interagency civilian expeditionary corps at DoD seems to be in conflict with that organization's support for building an interagency civilian expeditionary corps at the State Department, namely the Civilian Response Corps. The DUSD(CPP) also expressed a desire for OPM to play a greater role in helping to solve

---

[36] Gates, 2009.

[37] Stephen Losey, "Next up to Deploy: Civilians; DoD Assembles a Ready Cadre of Specialists," *Federal Times*, November 3, 2008.

[38] Losey, 2008.

interagency challenges.[39] It should be noted that OPM chairs and DoD is a member of the executive steering committee for the National Security Professional Development Program, which is designed to build a cadre of U.S. government civilians who are better prepared to address interagency challenges, as discussed in the next section.

Non-DoD Civilians at DoD: Joint Interagency Coordination Groups, SOUTHCOM, and AFRICOM

In addition to improving the deployable capacity of its civilians, DoD has also sought to increase interagency civilian presence in its COCOMs. This started in early 2002 with the creation in each of the COCOMs of Joint Interagency Coordination Groups (JIACGs) focused on counterterrorism. Initially, DoD reimbursed the Department of State, the Office of Foreign Assets Control in the Department of the Treasury, and the Federal Bureau of Investigation for sending representatives. The scope of the JIACGs was expanded in 2003 to include all missions, not just counterterrorism.

The JIACGs provide a useful tool for Combatant Commanders to experiment with interagency representation in their commands. Some groups have been more successful than others. Most have had a difficult time attracting interagency representatives beyond those reimbursed by DoD. The exceptions have been JIACGs in U.S. Northern Command and SOUTHCOM. Their role in domestic disaster response and counterdrug missions has eased coordination with representatives of other agencies. In fact, SOUTHCOM's long history with interagency operations dates back to the creation of Joint Interagency Task Force–South in 1989.

AFRICOM and SOUTHCOM built on the experience of the JIACGs to organize (or, in AFRICOM's case, create) themselves into more interagency-friendly commands and reflect those of their operations that are oriented more toward soft power. Rather than placing interagency representatives in a specialized group, they created interagency positions throughout their commands, including decisionmaking positions. Both AFRICOM and SOUTHCOM have a high-level civilian

---

[39] Losey, 2008.

deputy to the commander for civilian-military issues. These changes make AFRICOM and SOUTHCOM somewhat more attractive to interagency personnel, although actual staffing continues to lag.

The creation of AFRICOM along these lines sparked serious debate. Officials throughout the government were concerned that AFRICOM's new interagency structure and conflict-prevention focus were an attempt to move interagency decisionmaking on regional issues from Washington to the field and put it under the control of a military commander instead of State Department officials working with ambassadors and their staffs in the region. To allay these worries, DoD has emphasized that AFRICOM will play a supporting role to the State Department in promoting overall foreign-policy goals. There was less concern about SOUTHCOM's reorganization, perhaps because it was clear from the beginning that the scope of that COCOM's responsibilities would remain unchanged.

DoD's focus on COCOMs as the locus of interagency activity may be solipsistic. DoD is the only organization that has regional commands. Most organizations and agencies employ staff both in Washington (to coordinate regional issues and activities through the NSC process) and in the field (as representatives on country teams led by the COM to implement programs as needed). Among these organizations is DoD, which has regional staff in the Office of the Secretary of Defense and the Joint Staff and a senior defense official[40] on each country team. COCOMs sit in between the NSC process in Washington and the country team in the field. It makes sense for DoD to have operational-level regional organizations, such as the COCOMs, given its role in responding to crises. However, to the extent that DoD is involved in preventing crisis through long-term engagement with countries, the locus of effort should be at the country-team level in support of the COM. That said, as the State Department and USAID build up their crisis-response capabilities, continued engagement with COCOM planning staffs will be essential.

---

[40] The position of senior defense official was created in U.S. Department of Defense, Directive 5107.75, *Department of Defense Operations at U.S. Embassies*, December 21, 2007.

Remaining Challenges

Almost all of the key policy challenges of the last eight years have been interagency challenges, including stabilization and reconstruction, homeland security, and intelligence reform. The result has been a plethora of interagency strategies, priorities, and ideas with few attempts at rationalization. This means that there is no clear prioritization of interagency missions or potential contingencies to help drive resource allocation and capability development. These challenges can be addressed within the executive branch; however, changes in the legislative branch are needed as well. Congressional committees are not well structured to oversee or resource interagency missions. In addition to these interagency challenges, the U.S. government's federal structure and lack of a national police force create a capability gap specific to reconstruction and stabilization operations.

Prioritizing Interagency Missions and Contingencies

The increase in interagency challenges over the past eight years has also led to an increase in interagency organizations, such as S/CRS, the National Counterterrorism Center, DHS, and the Office of the Director of National Intelligence. To solve the particular interagency challenge assigned to them, each of these organizations had to address the common challenges associated with working in the interagency community. Rather than address interagency reform holistically, each organization developed its own strategies, plans, processes, and procedures. While experimenting with different approaches may have been useful initially, it has also created inefficiencies.

For example, there are no clear priorities among the various interagency strategies, plans, and priorities. Instead, departments and agencies are faced with a plethora of interagency strategies and plans and two lists of contingency priorities approved by the President.[41] Understand-

---

[41] The list of domestic incidents is called the National Planning Scenarios and is used for interagency planning (see Homeland Security Presidential Directive/HSPD-8, *National Preparedness*, Annex I). The list of military contingencies is part of a DoD document called *Guidance for the Employment of the Force* and is used for planning within DoD. Some military plans are coordinated with the interagency community.

ing the relative priority of various interagency challenges and contingencies, including stabilization and reconstruction, is essential to allocating scarce resources. To date, no attempt has been made to determine U.S. government priorities across different interagency areas (such as whether building civilian capacity for stabilization and reconstruction should be a higher priority than preparing for a domestic emergency).

Similarly, there are no common processes and procedures for developing interagency plans. Instead, there are at least two how-to guides on interagency planning, including S/CRS's planning framework,[42] as well as a number of interagency plans.[43] As a result, any organization that participates in interagency planning has to learn two similar but slightly different planning processes as well as those procedures and processes specific to existing interagency plans.

Military-Civilian Personnel and the Funding Mismatch

The State Department and USAID are often the first choices to lead stabilization and reconstruction operations. However, they often lack the capacity to lead and staff such operations, which require the ability to quickly deploy personnel and resources. When stability operations coincide with a military deployment, which they generally do, DoD and military personnel have repeatedly stepped in to fill the void. This was true during World War II[44] and remains true today.[45] As discussed

---

[42] The other is DHS's Integrated Planning System. While these two planning guides address different substantive issues, they overlap in the ways that they address interagency planning processes and functions.

[43] For example, the National Implementation Plan, the National Infrastructure Protection Plan, the National Response Framework, the National Strategy for Pandemic Influenza Implementation Plan, and the National Plan for Maritime Domain Awareness.

[44] The Department of State was the lead for postwar planning from 1941 to 1943. War Department planning began in 1943 and led to the establishment of military governments in Germany and Japan. See James Dobbins, Michele A. Poole, Austin Long, and Benjamin Runkle, *After the War*, Santa Monica, Calif.: RAND Corporation, MG-716-CC, 2008.

[45] NSPD-44 gives the State Department the lead for coordinating U.S. government stabilization and reconstruction efforts, and Directive 3000.05, *Military Support for Stability, Security, Transition, and Reconstruction (SSTR) Operations*, states that "U.S. military forces shall be prepared to perform all [stability operations] tasks necessary to maintain order when civilians cannot do so."

elsewhere in this book, this can lead to less-effective implementation of key stabilization and reconstruction tasks, to the detriment of the overall effort. Meanwhile, the perennial lack of capacity on the civilian side has resulted in what should be a rare contingency—the military taking the lead—becoming the default.

The primary reason it has been so consistently difficult to build civilian capacity is that the State Department and USAID, with the exception of OFDA, are not currently organized to respond rapidly to crises with large deployments of people. Their primary missions are to pursue U.S. foreign-policy interests and international development, which require a fundamentally different organizational structure than that of crisis response. Seeking to ensure capacity for both missions simultaneously creates tension and can raise questions about the organizations' primary mission. Every dollar of funding that goes to preparing for future eventualities is a dollar that is not being used to fund current diplomacy, security-assistance, and foreign-assistance programs. The reverse is true at DoD because its primary mission is to be prepared to respond to future eventualities. Every dollar used for engagement is a dollar not used to improve readiness. This is not to say that both sets of missions cannot live under the same roof—in USAID's case, they already do. However, establishing institutional mechanisms that let these missions cohabit effectively requires concerted design and effort.

Absent fundamental changes in organization and resources, the State Department and USAID will probably be more knowledgeable about stabilization and reconstruction issues than DoD but nowhere near as good at surging personnel in response to a crisis. Developing the capacity in civilian agencies to surge personnel and funding will need to be a key priority of senior U.S. leaders all the way up to the presidential level in order to spark changes in both capacity and organizational culture. The question is whether the State Department and USAID can develop and maintain the ability to surge personnel and funding in response to a crisis, or whether DoD will continue to be relied upon to undertake stabilization and reconstruction missions.

Congressional Committees

No fewer than eight separate congressional committees deal with stabilization and reconstruction issues. These committees cover the majority of legislation related to DoD, all of the legislation related to the State Department and USAID, and most legislation related to foreign aid. The reason for the proliferation of committees is that each issue is covered by both a standing committee and an appropriations subcommittee in both the House and the Senate. This means that for just two issues (i.e., defense and foreign affairs), there are eight congressional committees of importance:

- the Senate Armed Services Committee
- the House Armed Services Committee
- the Senate Appropriations Subcommittee on Defense
- the House Appropriations Subcommittee on Defense
- the Senate Foreign Affairs Committee
- the House Foreign Affairs Committee
- the Senate Appropriations Subcommittee on State, Foreign Operations, and Related Programs
- the House Appropriations Subcommittee on State, Foreign Operations, and Related Programs.

In general, the congressional-committee structure mirrors the executive-branch department and agency structure. Ironically, this means that Congress is often just as "stovepiped" as the executive branch, if not more so. As a result, stabilization and reconstruction issues, which require interagency cooperation, are challenging to manage in both the executive and legislative branches. Because different committees oversee the foreign affairs and defense budgets, the overall U.S. national security budget is never evaluated as a whole. The lack of deployable civilian capacity is rarely evaluated in the context of its implications for DoD, which makes it difficult to fully assess its operational consequences.

Even if departments and agencies in the executive branch can agree to a specific proposal, that is no guarantee that their respective congressional committees will agree. For the past three years, State and DoD have asked Congress to pass two legislative proposals known as

Sections 1206 and 1207. Section 1206 would allow DoD to reprogram its funds to train and equip foreign security forces with the approval of the Department of State. Section 1207 would allow DoD to transfer some of its funding to the State Department to support stabilization and reconstruction operations.

Both of these proposals involve joint oversight by State and DoD, and neither requires any new funding. They simply allow DoD to reprogram its funds. Nonetheless, it took a Herculean effort—including joint statements by the Secretaries of State and Defense—to get both proposals passed. Initially, the proposals were very unpopular. The committees dealing with defense issues were concerned about the proposal to shift DoD money elsewhere. On the other side, the committees dealing with foreign affairs preferred to have complete ownership and control of all foreign-affairs funding.

Congress could have chosen to shift money from DoD to the State Department, but this did not happen, partly because Congress is not set up to make funding trade-offs between committees. Congress is also not well organized to oversee programs managed by both State and DoD, such as those proposed in Sections 1206 and 1207. These programs encourage cooperation by requiring both State and DoD to agree before they can use the funding. In this way, they are similar to the UK's Conflict Prevention Pools, which are jointly managed by the Ministry of Defence, the Foreign & Commonwealth Office, and the Department for International Development. The UK's approach is much more comprehensive than are Sections 1206 and 1207, which are best described as pragmatic stopgap measures.

Constabulary Units and Stability Police

Constabulary and police units are critical to establishing security and the rule of law. They fill a critical niche between foreign militaries and civilian police organizations. The U.S. government does not have a federal police force. It has state and local police forces, a smattering of federal law-enforcement agents,[46] and military police. As a result, it is

---

[46] For example, the Federal Bureau of Investigation and Immigration and Customs Enforcement.

difficult for the U.S. government to deploy police forces abroad to stabilization and reconstruction missions.[47]

Currently, the United States can deploy individual volunteer police officers through a contract managed by the State Department. U.S. police officers have deployed to Iraq, Afghanistan, Haiti, Kosovo, Sudan, Lebanon, Liberia, and the Palestinian Authority.[48] The U.S. government does not have the capacity to deploy formed police units, with the partial exception of military police. However, military police are not well suited to stabilization and reconstruction missions. Their job is to police the military, and as a result, they are not trained to handle riots, looting, or large-scale violence, which are common in stabilization and reconstruction operations but not among military forces.

This is an enduring capability gap, both within the United States and worldwide. In the United States, state and local governments have few incentives to encourage police officers to serve abroad. It is unpopular to take a police officer away from protecting Americans and send him or her abroad to protect foreigners. Most police organizations do not have spare capacity to send abroad. A handful of other countries have constabulary or federal police that can deploy in formed units for stabilization and reconstruction scenarios.[49] However, these capabilities are in short supply because the forces are generally small in size and few countries have them.

The United States is working with allies and partners to help build police and constabulary capability abroad. In March 2005, Italy established a Center of Excellence for Stability Police Units (COESPU) in response to a Group of Eight action plan—proposed by the United States as part of its Global Peace Operations Initiative—concerned with expanding global capacity for peace-support operations. COESPU fol-

---

[47] For a good history of the United States and constabulary forces, see Robert Perito, *Where Is the Lone Ranger When We Need Him? America's Search for a Postconflict Stability Force*, Washington, D.C.: USIP Press Books, 2004.

[48] U.S. Department of State, "Fact Sheet: Civilian Police and Rule of Law Program," January 2, 2008.

[49] For example, Australia's Federal Police Force and Italy's *carabinieri*.

lows a "train-the-trainers" approach, so graduates of its program return home to train additional stability-police units. By mid-2008, COESPU had already trained 1,300 stability-police instructors and was on schedule to train a total of 3,000 instructors by 2010. Yet, mechanisms for tracking COESPU graduates are lacking, which means that it is not possible to determine how many have actually trained stability police in their home countries or how many have deployed on operations.[50] If these graduates do not effectively train police back home, it is hard to see how COESPU's efforts will significantly increase global capacity for stability policing.

Conclusion

The U.S. government has made substantial progress in addressing stabilization and reconstruction issues over the last eight years. Notable accomplishments include the creation of S/CRS and the subsequent development of concepts for planning and implementing stabilization and reconstruction operations. However, some key initiatives have fallen short. Efforts to develop a Civilian Response Corps have been stymied by a lack of funding from Congress. S/CRS has yet to develop a long-term, scenario-based plan (e.g., a deliberate plan) or even prioritize contingency scenarios. Requirements for jointness in the National Security Professional Development Program remain weak. In addition, a number of enduring challenges remain unresolved. Despite several organizational changes in the executive branch, such as the creation of DHS and the National Counterterrorism Center, the legislative branch has yet to alter its committee structure. The U.S. government continues to experience a shortage of forces that can perform constabulary or stability-police functions. Perhaps most importantly, while rhetoric about the importance of nonmilitary capabilities has grown, funding and capabilities have remained small compared to the challenge.

---

[50] U.S. Government Accountability Office, *Peacekeeping: Thousands Trained but United States Is Unlikely to Complete All Activities by 2010 and Some Improvements Are Needed*, GAO-08-754, June 26, 2008.

CHAPTER FOUR

Conclusions and Recommendations

Decisions about whether and how to develop capacity for stabilization and reconstruction in coming years should reflect U.S. foreign-policy priorities and goals. If the United States sees its foreign policy as best assured, at least in part, by helping to end conflict and promote development around the world, priority attention should be given to these issues. If the United States sees a smaller role for itself in nation-building around the world, then other issues can take center stage and a smaller capacity may be acceptable.

Most policy analysts believe that improved capacity is needed. Over the last eight years, many reports have been written on stabilization and reconstruction, and all agree on the need for increased civilian capacity and better interagency coordination. Moreover, the stabilization and reconstruction community is not alone in calling for increased civilian capacity and better interagency integration. Similar recommendations are made in reports on foreign-assistance reform, public diplomacy, strategic communications, terrorism, and homeland security. Despite agreement that better capabilities are needed, however, there is less consensus about how to go about achieving this goal, although most analysts agree about the general areas in which change is recommended. In *Surveying the Civilian Reform Landscape*, Craig Cohen and Noam Unger provide a good overview of civilian-reform recommendations and a matrix of reports and their recommendations.[1]

---

[1] Craig Cohen and Norm Unger, *Surveying the Civilian Reform Landscape*, The Stanley Foundation and the Center for a New American Security, 2008, Appendix A.

63

In this chapter, we suggest broad themes that should guide decisions about capacity development. We also identify ways to help reconcile priorities, resources, and capabilities in the years to come.

Emphasize Civilian Rather Than Military Capacity

As Chapter Three describes, much of the effort under way to develop capacity focuses on increasing deployable civilian capacity. However, U.S. military doctrine and training reflect a significant effort in the Pentagon to develop stabilization and reconstruction capabilities in the armed forces and DoD. As noted in Chapter Three, DoD is improving its own deployable civilian capacity in addition to incorporating stability operations into the training and doctrine of military personnel.

These continuing efforts on the part of DoD have both near- and long-term implications. DoD resources, mission, and capabilities give the organization a significant leg up over other U.S. government agencies in terms of being able to move quickly and effectively. Even as the armed forces have already incorporated aspects of stabilization and reconstruction into their guidance and missions, DoD's civilian deployment capacity may grow, at least in size, faster than the deployment capacity of civilian agencies. If the development of stabilization and reconstruction capabilities in DoD continues to outpace the development of similar capabilities in State and USAID, DoD will continue to lead stabilization and reconstruction operations by default. This could cause a number of long-term problems.

If nation-building remains a foreign-policy priority for the United States but the majority of resources and capabilities for that priority are concentrated in DoD, that organization, which already has the military missions under its control, will become the lead agency for a major component of U.S. foreign policy. Such a development would weaken the role of the State Department, both at home and abroad. It would raise concerns about the weakening of civilian control over military policy and undermine U.S. diplomatic efforts around the world. In short, it would be a fundamental realignment of how the United States both sees itself and is seen globally.

Such developments would send a powerful signal worldwide that the United States views stabilization and reconstruction as defense tasks rather than as components of its broader foreign policy. This would strengthen perceptions that the United States considers the military its primary instrument of power; it could also make stabilization, reconstruction, and other development efforts appear subsidiary to military missions. Such interpretations could be detrimental to perceptions of U.S. aid efforts globally, which could come to be seen as precursors to or components of military action. The United States would also face difficulty working with NGOs and IOs around the world, which would distrust the military's leadership of such missions. It would also make it more difficult during such operations for the U.S. government to coordinate with governments whose civilians take the lead.

Such a realignment would also likely prove ineffective. As we have discussed, most knowledge and experience related to development or reconstruction issues lies in the civilian branches of government and outside of government. With NGOs and IOs distrustful, other civilian specialists likely questioning the mission, and State and USAID capacity dwindling as resources flow to DoD, stabilization and reconstruction efforts would be undertaken without appropriate information and guidance. Moreover, because warfighting will remain the primary mission of DoD, development tasks would probably be aligned to advance military goals rather than be objectives unto themselves. In the long term, there is little discrepancy between development needs and security objectives, but in the near term, there are many trade-offs. Without advocates for development aims, there is a strong danger of humanitarian and development principles falling by the wayside in pursuit of tactical military victories.

This is not to say that military forces and DoD should not play a role in stabilization and reconstruction operations. As discussed, there will be times when military personnel are the only ones in a position to take action. However, both for planning and implementation of stabilization and reconstruction efforts, consistent and effective coordination of DoD efforts with civilian agencies, including civilian agency oversight and control where appropriate, is key to ensuring effectiveness. Developing civilian capability should be a priority if the U.S. government views stability operations as a key foreign- and security-policy mission. The United States would be ill-served by relying on military capacity for these efforts. Moreover, the U.S. government should develop a better-integrated interagency approach that places civilian institutions and objectives in the lead. In that context, the U.S. government should evaluate some of the steps taken by DoD in recent years to ensure that DoD efforts align with the overall goal of developing civilian capabilities.

Realign NSC, State, and USAID Roles

The challenges of interagency coordination often lead to pressures to create new bureaucracies to take charge of a policy area. This was the logic behind the creation of S/CRS. However, as an office within the State Department, S/CRS's ability to take charge of stabilization and reconstruction has been limited. This has led some to suggest alternative organizational structures. One frequently proposed solution is to move S/CRS, the governing structure for stabilization and reconstruction, into the NSC. Because the NSC's mission is to perform coordination within the U.S. government, an NSC-based S/CRS would have an easier time with that aspect of its mission. However, the NSC is not an implementing organization, so it would continue to rely on other agencies for everything except coordination. Another common suggestion is to create a new department or agency that would implement stabilization and reconstruction policies and programs. However, it is hard to imagine the United States creating a new Department of Nation Building. Doing so would draw unpleasant parallels to earlier ages of imperialism[2] and may not solve the problems identified in this book. A new bureaucracy would either have tremendous overlap with existing functions throughout the U.S. government or would have to consolidate such functions. Clearly, the model of drawing on capaci-

---

[2] See Max Boot, "Washington Needs a Colonial Office," *Financial Times*, July 3, 2003, and U.S. House of Representatives, Committee on Armed Services, *Panel on Roles and Missions: Initial Perspectives*, January 2008, pp. 45–47.

ties from a broad range of agencies has been problematic. But building new institutions would require both substantial resources and massive governmental initiatives.

While rearranging organizational charts is tempting, reforming existing organizations may make more sense and better utilize actual resources and capabilities. For example, one of the primary missions of the NSC is interagency coordination for foreign and security policy. It makes sense for the NSC to be responsible for interagency coordination for stabilization and reconstruction as a subset of that mission. However, the NSC is poorly resourced and structured to define detailed strategies and policies. This is an area in which the State Department and S/CRS may be better suited to play a role. The State Department has little large-scale expeditionary capability, and it does not control the majority of the programs and capabilities necessary to actually conduct stabilization and reconstruction operations. This would limit its ability to lead such operations in the field.

USAID does have an expeditionary culture (although it is limited to DCHA), and it controls the majority of programs related to stabilization and reconstruction. USAID is the organization that makes most sense, on the surface, to take the lead for stabilization and reconstruction operations. USAID was, after all, created to carry out many of these tasks, albeit on a smaller scale than is called for today. However, USAID and its parent organization, the State Department, have faced challenges when seeking to guide stabilization and reconstruction efforts, as the S/CRS experience has shown. USAID would require significant upgrading and development of capabilities, both functionally and organizationally, in order to take on leadership, just as the NSC and State Department require reforms to take on coordination and policy-definition tasks, respectively.

The key task in building civilian capacity is upgrading USAID and giving it the capability to be the lead agency for these missions in a way that aligns with and does not overtake its existing mandate. This will require transformation of recruiting, training, management, and deployment, but such change can draw on some of the reform efforts that are already in place (such as those implemented in DCHA). The goal is to make operational planning, action, deployment, and the ability to draw on capabilities from elsewhere fast and effective. In most cases, it will make sense for programs related to stabilization and reconstruction to remain in their current locations. In some cases, however, it might make sense to move programs to USAID. When new programs or initiatives related to stabilization and reconstruction are developed, such as the Civilian Response Corps, it will make sense to place them within USAID.

The State Department and NSC will play critical roles and must also be part of this effort to build capacity, but USAID is where the bulk of capacity fits best. The NSC can certainly play an important interagency-coordination role, and it will likely need to do so as USAID capacity is developed. The State Department can play a role in developing longer-term strategies and policies to support USAID-led operations. The division of responsibility between the State Department and USAID could be modeled on the relationship between DoD headquarters and the COCOMs. However, the lead needs to be understood and placed squarely in a foreign assistance—as opposed to military— context.

Fundamentally, stabilization and reconstruction are foreign-assistance missions, and the U.S. government's foreign-assistance agency should be responsible for them. There is a new recognition within the U.S. government that foreign assistance is critical to national-security goals. However, this does not mean that foreign-assistance efforts should be subordinate to traditional security goals. Rather, the U.S. government should recognize that traditional national-security tools and approaches should be brought into concert with foreign-assistance missions. This is what will assure security in the long term.

Fund and Implement the Civilian Stabilization Initiative

Chapter Three describes the key elements of the Civilian Stabilization Initiative, which is designed to include active, standby, and reserve corps of deployable civilian capacity. However, this initiative has never been fully funded. President George W. Bush's FY09 budget request includes $248 million for the initiative, but as of this writing, the pending legislation would appropriate only $115 million. The Obama administration should work closely with Congress to convince the relevant appropriations committees that relatively small investments in programs such as the Civilian Stabilization Initiative will provide large returns by ensuring that the U.S. government can adequately respond to the strategic challenges of stabilization and reconstruction.

Yet, funding is only the first step. Once adequate funds have been appropriated, a number of bureaucratic challenges associated with implementation will arise, especially regarding trade-offs with capacity at the state and local levels. The Reconstruction and Stabilization Civilian Management Act of 2008 includes an important caveat, stating that

> the establishment and deployment of any Civilian Reserve Corps shall be undertaken in a manner that will avoid substantively impairing the capacity and readiness of any State and local governments from which Civilian Reserve Corps personnel may be drawn.[3]

The implications of this language are not fully understood. For instance, an emergency similar to Hurricane Katrina or wildfires in California could mean that some or all of the Civilian Response Corps would not be available for reconstruction and stabilization operations abroad. In part, this is a force-sizing issue. Should the U.S. government have enough capacity to surge for simultaneous domestic and international crises? Or, should it take a risk and build only enough capacity to manage either a domestic or an international crisis?

This is also a management issue. Determining what state and local resources could be available for international deployment without "substantially impairing" their capacity is a political question. Most state and local governments will say that any reduction in their resources would substantially impair their capacity and readiness. This issue arose during decisions to deploy National Guard units to Iraq. An interesting management model is USAID's development of USAR Teams for

---

[3] Public Law 110-417, Title XVI, The Reconstruction and Stabilization Civilian Management Act of 2008.

international deployments, which the Federal Emergency Management Agency replicated and expanded for domestic emergency response.[4]

Improve Deployable Police Capacity

Building effective deployable police capacity for both community policing and specialized high-end police tasks is a subset of developing overall deployable civilian capacity. This component, however, requires special attention because of its significant requirements in terms of both number of personnel and capabilities. Effective, trained police are often critical both for establishing law and order and training local law-enforcement personnel. As discussed in Chapter Two, there are no good alternatives to deploying such personnel—military forces simply have a different skill set, and foreign police capacity will rarely be available in the numbers needed for such operations. While MPs can and should be used in immediate stabilization efforts, we do not support redefining their mission to include the broader effort to provide policing and police training abroad.

As with civilian deployment overall, a structure that includes elements of the National Guard and Reserve model as well as USAID's model for USAR Teams may prove to be the right approach. Some current and former police officers may be amenable to participating in regular training (with the possibility of being deployed) to broaden their experience and earn additional income. Some, particularly former police, already do so, participating in international deployments as contractors for UN civilian police (CIVPOL) deployments. On a large scale, however, utilizing currently serving police officers presents problems. These officers are unlikely to be willing to undertake these commitments if, for example, their employers are not legally bound to hold their jobs for them while they are on deployment (as employers of Guard and Reserve personnel are). This is, of course, the case with all deployable civilians, but it may be particularly true in the case of police. City police forces, which often have significant personnel shortages, may not be willing

---

4   Feil et al., 2006.

to give up large numbers of personnel for either short-term training or (especially) long-term deployment, particularly if they can only replace these personnel with short-term hires.[5] USAID's model for USAR Teams may provide a useful starting point for solving these problems. Under this concept, the federal government would provide extra funding to state and local governments to develop "extra" police units with the caveat that these units have to be available for international deployment. When the units are not deployed, they would provide additional capacity to state and local police forces.

If the U.S. government is serious about expanding its deployable police capacity, it will need to find ways to encourage police departments around the country—as well as individual police officers themselves—to participate. The Guard, Reserve, and USAR Teams may serve as models, but success will require a comprehensive effort that unites the executive branch, Congress, and state and local governments in the search for a manageable solution that meets the needs of local law enforcement as well as national requirements.

The capacity for deploying police should be compatible with UN CIVPOL and other international police deployments. Police, no less than military or other civilian personnel, need to be able to effectively work with their foreign counterparts when deployed. Making U.S. police "reservists" available, on a voluntary basis and with suitable recompense, to UN CIVPOL and other international efforts can be useful for training and maintaining skills.

Improve Management for Stabilization and Reconstruction

The State Department and USAID have focused on improving day-to-day and strategic management,[6] but they have paid less attention

---

[5] This could, of course, be of particular concern in regards to specialized police, such as Special Weapons and Tactics (SWAT) officers.

[6] Until recently, the State and USAID strategic-planning processes were largely separate. In 2003, State and USAID developed their first joint strategic plan. In 2007, the first Direc-

to crisis management. Effective crisis management includes at least four elements: identifying potential missions, building capacity, planning for missions, and managing missions after they are launched (all described in more detail below). As discussed earlier, USAID may be in a better position to build capacity and plan and manage missions than the State Department or S/CRS. The State Department is well placed to identify potential missions, however, and it can support USAID efforts with budgetary and programmatic capacity, some of which can be transferred to USAID over time. The NSC is, of course, responsible for interagency coordination.

Identifying potential missions. As discussed in Chapter Three, the National Intelligence Council has developed an internal instability watchlist at the request of S/CRS. The countries on the list are ranked by their level of instability. However, the more important criterion from a management perspective is the likelihood that the U.S. government will become involved. There is little point in planning and preparing for missions in which the United States is unlikely to become involved. S/CRS should develop a prioritized list of interagency reconstruction and stabilization contingencies for approval by the NSC Principals Committee or Deputies Committee. In doing so, it should be sure to include prospective missions at various plausible levels of effort (based on requirements) and with various degrees of military involvement.

Building capacity. This book has emphasized the need to build civilian capacity for stabilization and reconstruction missions. From a management perspective, the key questions are how much capacity should be built and in which areas. There is no one right way to determine what the U.S. government needs and how to go about attaining it. Stabilization and reconstruction efforts will range in size and level of effort, and U.S. personnel are likely to be involved in a number of such efforts at any given time. Some will be large, some will be small; some will follow armed conflict, and some will take place in countries where most fighting ended some time ago. USAID and the State Department

---

tor of Foreign Assistance was appointed, effectively merging State and USAID foreign-assistance programs.

will need to integrate this capacity with their broader foreign-assistance efforts, ensuring that they are part and parcel of them.

A few approaches may make sense. One is to emulate the U.S. military's planning mechanism, which posits a steady-state capacity and capability to fight two simultaneous regional conflicts. This construct has proven problematic, however, in part because the military did not anticipate involvement lengthy conflicts, such as those in Iraq and Afghanistan. Another approach is to let current needs and requirements serve as the planning determinants, but this approach would need to be combined with some assessment of how requirements might increase or drop and how dialing back and surging could be accomplished. Various aid agencies' planning and sizing approaches could be looked at as models. Fundamentally, however, the agencies responsible for most of the work, in this case USAID and the State Department, should be the ones who determine how they will assess needs and create capacities to deal with them.

Planning for missions. Contingency plans describe how an organization will use its capabilities in a crisis. S/CRS has spent considerable time developing planning tools, such as the Planning Framework for Reconstruction, Stabilization and Conflict Transformation, and planning for ongoing operations. However, this has come at the expense of spending time to develop plans for future missions. S/CRS has not yet developed any contingency plans. S/CRS has repeatedly committed itself to developing a prioritized list of contingency plans, but actually doing so has been continually delayed to allow the office to pursue more-pressing priorities. This is a classic management problem: Preparing for future missions and crises almost always loses out to the crisis of the day. State Department and S/CRS leadership should monitor this process to ensure that planning for potential missions actually happens, whether at S/CRS or USAID.

Managing missions after they are launched. S/CRS has put a lot of work into developing concepts, like the IMS, that describe how it would manage a crisis. The key is to move from concept to reality. S/CRS is currently writing chapters for each part of the IMS. This is a good first step, but the key will be identifying the personnel and resources needed to get each of the concepts up and running. In many cases, this will probably require memorandums of agreement between various departments and agencies.

Improving crisis management for stabilization and reconstruction in each of the four areas discussed above is a good first step. The next step is to improve crisis management for a range of interagency issues, both international and domestic, while leveraging related efforts at DHS[7] and the National Counterterrorism Center.

Ensure Coherent Guidance and Funding for Effectiveness and Sustainability

Building capacity for stabilization and reconstruction means not only developing the right approach but also making sure that approach can be implemented. This means that the legal and bureaucratic framework has to reflect efforts under way, that resources must be allocated as needed, and that the institutions created can outlast individual administrations. The specifics of how this is done matter less than the requirement for collaboration between the key agencies and the U.S. Congress (and, as noted, local and state governments in many cases) to ensure that capacity development is treated as a national-security priority.

Such directives as NSPD-44 are important, but they are themselves insufficient. Presidential-level guidance must be the source of a coherent and consistent package of regulations and rules that create an effective new system. Furthermore, this package should be developed in coordination with congressional guidance in terms of both defining missions and tasks and allocating resources.

Without the appropriate resources, it will not be possible to do what is required. If resources do not go to the right place, and must be shifted around, effectiveness will be compromised. Resource allocations in line with overall guidance on division of labor and leadership roles will cement these capabilities in the bureaucracy. This, in turn,

---

[7] The DHS has developed National Planning Scenarios (which identify crises), an Integrated Planning System (which helps the organization plan), a National Preparedness Goal (which helps the organization prepare), and a National Incident Management System (which helps the organization manage).

is needed to ensure long-term sustainability. The current imbalance between funding and authority undermines efforts to build civilian capacity and creates inefficiencies. It also makes it entirely too easy to overturn current approaches and initiatives.

What is needed is a clearer mandate[8] and more direct funding for USAID and the State Department to ensure that capacity can be built, used, and sustained. A more enduring division of labor is needed among the U.S. government agencies involved in stabilization and reconstruction so that these organizations have incentives to make long-term investments in the areas for which they are responsible. This division of labor will take time to enact. In the meantime, it will be tempting, and at times necessary, to take steps that fix the symptoms but not the disease. For instance, the State Department's Bureau of International Narcotics and Law Enforcement Affairs (INL) account has historically been used primarily for counternarcotics issues. It is also the only account at present that can be used for training prosecutors, judges, and foreign police forces. This makes it a de facto stabilization and reconstruction account. In the near term, building up police training capacity by definition means building up this fund and improving INL's capacity to use it. In the long term, however, the substantial demands of stabilization and reconstruction on this source of funding mean that a better solution, with clearer mandates, should be developed. A balance should be struck between policy steps that are needed to respond to immediate needs and those that must be developed for long-term effectiveness.

One additional mechanism that could help ensure that funds can be appropriately allocated and spent would be a congressional funding line for stabilization and reconstruction (potentially as a component of foreign assistance) shared by the State Department, USAID, and DoD. The United Kingdom's conflict-response fund could be a model. Under such a system, funds for efforts in which all three agencies play an important role could be divided up between those agencies accord-

---

[8]   For example, the roles and responsibilities of various departments and agencies for domestic emergency response are outlined in Public Law 100-707, Robert T. Stafford Disaster Relief and Emergency Assistance Act, November 23, 1988.

ing to requirements. The system could also support collaborative and cooperative training and planning efforts among the three agencies. It could not, however, take the place of a clear delineation of responsibilities and the provision of resources that make it possible for these agencies to fulfill their responsibilities.

Bibliography

BearingPoint, *Management Study for Establishing a Civilian Reserve*, May 2006.

Bensahel, Nora, "Organising for Nation Building," *Survival*, Vol. 49, No. 2, Summer 2007, pp. 43–76.

Boot, Max, "Washington Needs a Colonial Office," *Financial Times*, July 3, 2003.

Buvinic, Mayra, and Andrew R. Morrison, "Introduction, Overview, and Future Policy Agenda," in Mayra Buvinic, Andrew R. Morrison, A. Waafas Ofosu-Amaah, and Mirja Sjöblom, eds., *Equality For Women: Where Do We Stand on Equality Development Goal 3?* Washington, D.C.: The International Bank for Reconstruction and Development/The World Bank, 2008.

Cohen, Craig, and Norm Unger, *Surveying the Civilian Reform Landscape*, The Stanley Foundation and the Center for a New American Security, 2008.

Convention (IV) Relative to the Protection of Civilian Persons in Time of War, Geneva, August 12, 1949.

Crane, Keith, Olga Oliker, Nora Bensahel, Derek Eaton, S. Jamie Gayton, Brooke Stearns Lawson, Jeffrey Martini, John L. Nasir, Michelle Parker, Jerry M. Sollinger, and Kayla M. Williams, *Guidebook for Providing Economic Assistance at the Tactical Level During Stability Operations*, Santa Monica, Calif.: RAND Corporation, TR-633-A, 2009. As of March 10, 2009:
http://www.rand.org/pubs/technical_reports/TR633/

Dobbins, James, Seth G. Jones, Keith Crane, and Beth Cole DeGrasse, *The Beginner's Guide to Nation Building*, Santa Monica, Calif.: RAND Corporation, MG-557-SRF, 2007. As of February 16, 2008:
http://www.rand.org/pubs/monographs/MG557/

Dobbins, James, Michele A. Poole, Austin Long, and Benjamin Runkle, *After the War*, Santa Monica, Calif.: RAND Corporation, MG-716-CC, 2008. As of February 16, 2008:
http://www.rand.org/pubs/monographs/MG716/

Executive Order 13434, *National Security Professional Development*, May 17, 2007.

Feil, Scott, et al., *Joint Interagency Evaluation: Civil Reconstruction and Stabilization Reaction Force*, Washington, D.C.: Institute for Defense Analysis, August 2006.

Flournoy, Michèle, "Interagency Strategy and Planning for Post-Conflict Reconstruction," in Robert C. Orr, ed., *Winning the Peace: An American Strategy for Post-Conflict Reconstruction*, Washington, D.C.: Center for Strategic and International Studies, 2004.

Gates, Robert M., "A Balanced Strategy: Reprogramming the Pentagon for a New Age," *Foreign Affairs*, Vol. 88, No. 1, January/February 2009.

Ghani, Ashraf, and Clare Lockhart, *Fixing Failed States: A Framework for Rebuilding a Fractured World*, Oxford, UK: Oxford University Press, 2008.

Global Facilitation Network for Security Sector Reform, *A Beginner's Guide to Security Sector Reform*, Birmingham, UK, 2007.

Gompert, David C., Olga Oliker, and Anga Timilsina, *Clean, Lean and Able: A Strategy for Defense Sector Development*, Santa Monica, Calif.: RAND Corporation, OP-101-RC, 2004. As of February 16, 2009: http://www.rand.org/pubs/occasional_papers/OP101/

Hagman, Lotta, and Zoe Nielsen, *A Framework for Lasting Disarmament, Demobilization, and Reintegration of Former Combatants in Crisis Situations*, International Peace Academy IPA Workshop Report, December 31, 2002.

Headquarters, Department of the Army, Field Manual 3-24, *Counterinsurgency: The Army and Marine Corps Field Manual on Counterinsurgency*, December 2006.

———, Field Manual 3-0, *Operations*, February 2008.

———, Field Manual 3-07, *Stability Operations*, October 2008.

Huntington, Samuel P., *Political Order in Changing Societies*, New Haven, Conn.: Yale University Press, 1968.

International Committee of the Red Cross, "International Humanitarian Law," Web page, undated. As of January 16, 2009: http://www.icrc.org/web/eng/siteeng0.nsf/iwpList2/Humanitarian_law?OpenDocument

Joint Chiefs of Staff, Joint Publication 1-02, *DoD Dictionary of Military and Associated Terms*, April 12, 2001, as amended through October 17, 2008.

Joint Chiefs of Staff, Joint Publication 3-0, *Operations*, September 2006.

Kelly, Terrence K., Ellen E. Tunstall, Thomas S. Szayna, and Deanna Weber Prine, *Stabilization and Reconstruction Staffing: Developing U.S. Civilian Personnel Capabilities*, Santa Monica, Calif.: RAND Corporation, MG-580-RC, 2008. As of February 16, 2009: http://www.rand.org/pubs/monographs/MG580/

Losey, Stephen, "Next up to Deploy: Civilians; DoD Assembles a Ready Cadre of Specialists," *Federal Times*, November 3, 2008.

Muggah, Robert, "No Magic Bullet: A Critical Perspective on Disarmament, Demobilization and Reintegration (DDR) and Weapons Reduction in Post-Conflict Contexts," *The Round Table*, Vol. 94, No. 379, April 2005, pp. 239–252.

National Security Professional Development, *National Strategy for the Development of Security Professionals*, July 2007.

Perito, Robert, *Where Is the Lone Ranger When We Need Him? America's Search for a Postconflict Stability Force*, Washington, D.C.: USIP Press Books, 2004.

Pouligny, Béatrice, *The Politics and Anti-Politics of Contemporary "Disarmament, Demobilization & Reintegration" Programs*, Paris/New York/Geneva: CERI/SGDN/PSIS, September 2004.

Public Law 99-433, Title IV, Section 664, Length of Joint Duty Assignments, October 6, 1986.

Public Law 100-707, Robert T. Stafford Disaster Relief and Emergency Assistance Act, November 23, 1988.

Public Law 110-252, Supplemental Appropriations Act, 2008, June 30, 2008.

Public Law 110-417, Title XVI, The Reconstruction and Stabilization Civilian Management Act, July 14, 2008.

Protocol Additional to the Geneva Conventions of 12 August 1949, and relating to the Protection of Victims of International Armed Conflicts (Protocol I), June 8, 1977.

Protocol Additional to the Geneva Conventions of 12 August 1949, and relating to the Protection of Victims of Non-International Armed Conflicts (Protocol II), June 8, 1977.

Schnabel, Albrect, and Hans-Georg Ehrhart, eds., *Security Sector Reform and Post-Conflict Peacebuilding*, Tokyo: United Nations University Press, 2005.

Secretary of State Condoleezza Rice, "Remarks on Foreign Assistance," January 19, 2006.

Stevenson, Charles A., *Warriors and Politicians: US Civil-Military Relations Under Stress*, New York: Routledge, 2006.

Szayna, Thomas S., Derek Eaton, James E. Barnett II, Brooke Stearns Lawson, Terrence K. Kelly, and Zachary Haldeman, *Integrating Civilian Agencies in Stability Operations*, Santa Monica, Calif.: RAND Corporation, MG-801-A, forthcoming.

United Kingdom Department for International Development, *Understanding and Supporting Security Sector Reform*, London, 2002.

United Nations Interagency Working Group on Disarmament, Demobilization, and Reintegration, "Briefing Note for Senior Managers on the Integrated Disarmament, Demobilization, and Reintegration Standards," undated. As of December 2008:
http://www.unddr.org/

United Nations Peacekeeping, "Monthly Summary of Contributors of Military and Civilian Police Personnel, 2009," Web page, 2009. As of February 16, 2009:
http://www.un.org/Depts/dpko/dpko/contributors/

United States Institute of Peace, *Guidelines for Relations Between U.S. Armed Forces and Non-Governmental Humanitarian Organizations in Hostile or Potentially Hostile Environments*, c. 2007.

U.S. Agency for International Development, *A Guide to Economic Growth in Post-Conflict Countries*, Washington, D.C., 2008.

U.S. Department of Defense, Directive 3000.05, *Military Support for Stability, Security, Transition, and Reconstruction (SSTR) Operations*, November 28, 2005.

———, Directive 5107.75, *Department of Defense Operations at U.S. Embassies*, December 21, 2007.

U.S. Department of State, "Fact Sheet: The Civilian Response Corps of the United States of America," July 16, 2008.

———, "Fact Sheet: Civilian Police and Rule of Law Program," January 2, 2008.

———, *Foreign Assistance Framework*, July 10, 2007.

———, *Summary and Highlights: International Affairs Function 150, Fiscal Year 2009 Budget Request*, undated.

U.S. Government Accountability Office, *Peacekeeping: Thousands Trained but United States Is Unlikely to Complete All Activities by 2010 and Some Improvements Are Needed*, GAO-08-754, June 26, 2008.

U.S. House of Representatives, Committee on Armed Services, *Panel on Roles and Missions: Initial Perspectives*, January 2008.

U.S. Senate, S.3288, Department of State, Foreign Operations, and Related Programs Appropriations Act, 2009, July 18, 2008.

The White House, Homeland Security Presidential Directive/HSPD-8, *National Preparedness*, December 17, 2003.

———, National Security Presidential Directive/NSPD-44, *Management of Interagency Efforts Concerning Reconstruction and Stabilization*, December 7, 2005.

———, Presidential Decision Directive/PDD-56, *Managing Complex Contingency Operations*, May 1997.

World Bank, "Promoting Gender Equality and Women's Empowerment," in World Bank, *Global Monitoring Report 2007: Millennium Development Goals: Confronting the Challenges of Gender Equality and Fragile States*, Washington, D.C.: World Bank, 2007.